GUIDED BY
THE LIGHT

GUIDED BY THE LIGHT

The Autobiography of a Born Medium

Philip Solomon

APEX PUBLISHING LTD

First published in 2008 by
Apex Publishing Ltd
PO Box 7086, Clacton on Sea, Essex, CO15 5WN

www.apexpublishing.co.uk

Copyright © 2008 by Philip Solomon
The author has asserted his moral rights

British Library Cataloguing-in-Publication Data
A catalogue record for this book
is available from the British Library

ISBN 1-906358-03-6   978-1-906358-03-7

Typeset in 10pt Times New Roman

Production Manager: Chris Cowlin

Cover Design: Siobhan Smith

Printed and bound in Great Britain

*Dedicated to Kath, my wife, lover,
the mother of my children and,
undoubtedly, my best friend.*

Two of my favourite quotations:

*"If you want to know the past,
Look at your present life.
If you want to know the future,
Look at your present."*
- GAUTAMA BUDDHA

*"I do not ask for any crown
But that which all may win;
Nor try to conquer any world
Except the one within.
Be thou my guide until I find
Led by a tender hand,
The happy kingdom in myself
And dare to take command."*
- LOUISA MAY ALCOTT

Foreword
by Derek Acorah

It was with the greatest of pleasure that I accepted Philip Solomon's invitation to add my "bit" in the form of a foreword to his latest book "Guided by the Light: The Autobiography of a Born Medium".

I often look back with pleasure to the time when I first met Philip Solomon. I was a weekly contributor to a programme "Psychic Livetime", aired live by Granada Breeze, the then satellite arm of Granada Television in Manchester. Each week various guest contributors would be invited to take part in the show. Some were good, some were not so good and then there was Philip! I was instantly drawn to his warmth as a human being and his prodigious mediumistic gift. I recognised within him a special spiritual light and deeply appreciated the dedication he showed to his work for the spirit world. As we worked together, side by side, I was joyous in the knowledge that I was with a true master. I was at last working with somebody who was as committed to their work for spirit as I was myself. It is obvious that Philip's gifts were also recognised by the viewing public, as he was invited back to the programme on a number of occasions.

Philip is an accomplished writer and broadcaster. He achieves a perfect blend of inspirational words with sound commonsense. Through his works he has assisted in dispelling the apprehension of those mystified by such things as clairvoyance, clairaudience and their associated subjects. In his own inimitable way, Philip assists us in expanding spiritually and gaining a greater understanding of the world of spirit. It is his wise words in the form of his various writings, and particularly his weekly column in "The Psychic News", that have given me assistance in my ponderings of all things spiritual... and some things not so spiritual!

I have the deepest respect for Philip Solomon both as a man and as a medium and I look forward to the day when I can once again work with him on a project.

Derek Acorah
International Medium, TV Presenter & Author

Contents

Introduction

I was born, or should I say, I chose to enter this life on 23rd July 1951, the only child of two loving parents, both exceptionally psychic. My mother, in particular, was to be my mentor, friend, teacher and protector. She had seen a lot of ups and downs and could quickly call upon life's experience to answer almost any question. A committed Spiritualist and medium, mom also hung on to the ethics of traditional church values, always seeing her work as the work of Jesus. She had many clients from the very famous to ordinary old ladies who seemed very poor indeed to me, but she never took a penny from any of them for her gifts, even when money was really tight.

She was also a strict disciplinarian, yet a very down-to-earth lady in many ways. She knew I was psychic, probably even before I could talk, but never let anything or anyone frighten me with actions or talk I would not understand in my affirmative years. I remember, at about two years of age, seeing an old lady sitting in a rocking chair that no one else could see except my mother, who explained the situation matter-of-factly to the old lady and she left residence in that house. (She did come back some years later, however!) I also clearly remember talking to another old lady when I was about three in our front room. She seemed to be suspended about two feet off the ground.

"Hello. Who are you?" I asked.

"Can you see me, son?" asked the lady, adjusting her white shawl.

"Of course I can," I answered.

"Well, son, you could say I am your great grandmamma." And with a smile she simply faded away.

I rushed to the kitchen to tell my mother what I had seen. Surprisingly, she told me it was only my imagination, yet in later years she admitted the description perfectly fitted her grandmother. Apparently she felt at that time she had to make sure I didn't develop psychically too fast and end up being scared. After all, I was only three years of age!

I also recall lying in bed one night and seeing on the bedroom wall what my young eyes perceived to be a firework with the most beautiful colours that rose up and formed the shape of a tree. Of course, I now realise this was a vision of the Tree of Life. Other experiences as a little boy included seeing Red Indians, one in particular who was to become a future guide of mine, and has also been seen by my wife. There were Chinamen and people that today I would describe as of Mandarin origin and, to be honest, they used to scare me even though I am quite sure they never intended to. I also once had a dream in which an Indian chief and a brave came to my bedside and covered me with a tartan blanket, smiled and then walked away. Strangely enough, I enjoyed that dream and woke up happy and contented.

Returning to my mother's background, what a hard life she had. The eldest of six children, born of my grandfather Will, a platelayer on the railway, and my grandmother Mary, sometimes cleaner and washerwoman of other people's dirty clothes as well as that of her own family and, at other times, opera singer, show-woman and, so I am led to believe, a very good medium. These part-time vocations must have been difficult, for grandfather was a straight-laced, orthodox, Victorian-type character, who was not given to the appreciation of such arts! I never knew my grandfather and I was only about two when my grandmother gave up on this life, but whenever I look at my Equity card I always think of her. Mother fell in love at 20 years of age and married a man named Leslie, whom she loved deeply all her life. Unfortunately, this man contracted tuberculosis and passed to the higher life at the age of 28, leaving my mother, in her words, devastated. She always claimed that Spiritualism kept her sane and she went on to serve that religion as a medium, church member, president and worker all her life, despite suffering from very poor health all her life. I never really remember a time when my mother wasn't very ill or in hospital. In fact, twice when I was a boy I was warned that my mother might die. I think I was eight at the time when I said to my dad and aunt, "She won't, you know. My mom's staying with me until I am grown up."

But let me return to her life before I was born. When she was 34 she met my dad, an ex-staff sergeant in the Parachute Regiment and as dapper a little character as you could ever wish to meet! Mom was lonely and my dad wanted to marry her. In earlier years my mother had been the most beautiful girl imaginable and was still very attractive, whereas dad was a fairly ordinary sort of chap, but Karma being what it is they married and for two years they tried desperately to have a child but to no avail. Many visits to doctors and specialists followed and eventually mother was informed she could not have children. She said she was heartbroken but just got on with her life and submerged herself in work and the Spiritualist Church and this is where one night she received a message from a young medium named Gordon Higginson, a man who one day would become president of the whole National Spiritualist Church movement.

"Elsie, I want to come to you," he said to my mother. "Do you know you are having a baby?"

"I wouldn't think so, Gordon," she replied. "I can't have children."

The medium insisted that he was right. "This is a boy who will speak to the world and he will stand on this very platform in this very church."

"I don't see it," said my mother.

"We'll see the next time we meet then."

Fanny Higginson, Gordon's mother, knew mom and insisted that her son was right. But mother was a medium herself and felt the message must have another meaning. Perhaps her mediumistic ability or pride had been slightly pricked. Whatever the case, she left church early that night and for the next few weeks just got on with living her life. By now, dad had become a dance hall promoter and this was the time of, or should I say the birth of, rock 'n' roll music. He had seen its fatal attraction for the post-war teenagers of that time and really he should have made a million rather than the millions he was to put in the path of other entrepreneurs! But, there again, perhaps that was not his way in this life.

One evening my father returned home to find my mother feeling very sick and looking really ill. An appointment was made for a visit to the family doctor, a lady called Doctor Madison, who after two more visits declared to my mother, "Elsie, my dear, you are pregnant, but of course we shall have to terminate this pregnancy."

Mother was quiet for a few seconds, remembering Gordon Higginson's prediction.

Doctor Madison continued, "There is no way you could carry a baby. It would kill you and the child."

Without one moment of consideration my mother told the doctor, "I will have this baby, I don't care if it does kill me!"

"You most certainly will not," answered the doctor. "It is completely out of the question!"

Mother was deeply upset but determined. Shortly before this news, a young Scottish couple, Doctors Alfred and Ruth Russell, had joined the practice. My mother's sister, Bertha, suggested they go and see Doctor Ruth for a second opinion. Ruth Russell examined her and told her, "Times have changed, but truly there is not more than a fifty-fifty chance of you carrying a child full term." It also appeared to the two sisters that the young Doctor Ruth was in some awe of the senior partner, Doctor Madison, but they both pleaded and Ruth Russell finally agreed, "Let's give it a go."

Nine months later, I was born. Mom went through 36 hours of labour and very nearly did die, and her health was never very good afterwards, but she handed to me the most precious gift on earth - life! Doctor Madison, thenceforth, always insisted on calling me her 'little miracle child' and I must admit by the time I had reached about ten I had just about had enough of it and found it most embarrassing!

My time at school was spent in much the same way as any other boy but I never really enjoyed it. To be honest I always felt older than the other children and I know this sounds ungrateful and unkind but the teachers all seemed distant and at times I used to think, "These people know nothing that is of use to me. I wish I was in the country or the woods of my beloved Wales," a place where I spent much of my childhood years and where to me nature seemed more kindly, worthwhile and instructional than those teachers. But I needed an education to operate in the world and one lady at my secondary modern school, Mrs Booker, could get through to me and it is perhaps down to her that I left school just about literate and moved into the world of work!

I had all kinds of jobs, from working in factories and shops to playing in pop groups. I always wanted to move on and change as soon as I had got the grasp of any occupation and by now I was making use of my psychic abilities. At parties I would delight in telling the girls' fortunes or secrets - a sure-fire method of extra popularity with the opposite sex! I suppose by then I was about eighteen years old. One of my friends was an Indian lad named Darshan but we all knew him as Bill. He had an older brother who had an amazing knowledge of two subjects that fascinated me: meditation and hypnosis. I was drawn like a magnet to his methods of hypnosis. I wanted to know all his secrets and within a few months I did. In fact, I was better, much better, than him. I know that sounds big-headed but it's the truth!

Now at parties and social gatherings not only could I tell fortunes, I could hypnotise as well. But I never did anything wrong with the skill except on one occasion when this really arrogant guy gave me a bad time, along the lines that no one could hypnotise him and all the psychic stuff I talked about was utter rot. I hypnotised him and told him he was a cockerel and duly forgot him for two hours. When I did remember him, he had been bent over like a bird for a very long time. I awakened him from the hypnotic state and it was obvious that his back was giving him some trouble. Quick as a flash I re-hypnotised him and told him he had slightly strained his back while playing rugby, a game that he played regularly. I saw him a couple of days later and luckily all was well.

Mother was always saying, "Philip, why do you always waste your gifts the way you do?" But I was a teenager, with abilities that others did not possess and fun was the operative word at that time of my life!

The next important stage in my life saw me meet my wife to be, Kath. We really liked each other as soon as we met and she has always insisted that as soon as she saw me she knew we would be together. I felt much the same about her and my parents adored her, especially my mother, who took to her as if she were a daughter straight away, and yet with Kath's parents and me it was just the opposite - natural dislike. In fact, at times her mother would make life unbearable. Still, we all have our Karma to work out, but unfortunately at that time I didn't particularly understand the fact.

Never mind, Kath and I were happy and within a year we married and had our first child whom we named Nadine. We were desperately hard up for money and I seemed to have to work all the hours there were in a day, but somehow we always had just enough to get by. Eventually, my wife's parents lent us the money to buy a little house and my parents basically fed us, clothed us and, to be honest, did so much more it is hard to explain. I made the decision that it was time to go back to school - night classes at least. I loved it really, and found I had a high-speed ability to learn and pass as many examinations as I could and did so surprisingly easily in fact.

Strange as it seems, at that time I also kept meeting people who knew about psychic matters and they all encouraged me to develop my inherent psychic gifts. Two years on, I started to train at college to be a Welfare Officer, studying subjects such as sociology, social work practice, psychology, etc., all at honours degree level. Psychology I found fascinating, and my tutor, a brilliant psychologist, a lady named Rae Walter, taught me more than any other person outside my family the way of the world and the reason we react to it the way we do. The course also helped me in later life to decide what was psychic or a conditioned response or, indeed, simply mind over matter, if you like. Rae Walter also arranged a placement for me with the Rudolf Steiner movement and, again, much was to be discovered that would help me in the future. I never actually asked Rae, but I am pretty sure she knew I was someone she had just got to help and she did. While all this education was being taken on board, whenever I had any spare time I would seek to learn more about arts such as astrology, tarot and anything to do with psychic, spiritual and, in particular, mediumship development.

Mom always used to moan at me about getting involved in matters that she considered foolish and unworthy, but I had to know. I had to learn and I always did it my way. People just seemed to continue arriving in my life who would help me to learn what I needed to know fast. Within five years, I was the resident astrologer/stars columnist for a Midlands newspaper. By word of mouth and reputation, people were getting to know me from all over the world and by this time my psychic abilities were operating at a very high level of vibration and at last I was making some money. We needed it too, because by now another addition to the family had arrived, a little boy, Paul.

Kath and I were very happy, but let me tell you about a psychic experience I had for myself at that time. Kath, together with her mother, had seen a bungalow she really liked and wanted us to buy it. We talked it over but decided it was impossible; we just could not afford it. Even by selling our own home and borrowing or begging every penny we could raise, we would still be £3,600 short of the money required to change properties (a small fortune at that time). We went to bed one Wednesday evening very late, accepting that the bungalow was out of the question. Kath was clearly disappointed but secretly I was glad! I didn't want this bungalow; I didn't like where it was and I didn't really want to leave our small terraced home. But I was sorry for Kath because she really loved it.

That night, contented, I quickly fell asleep and dreamt that a man covered in leaves visited me; I often refer to him as 'the leafy man'. In my dream he led me to a gate where he instructed me to stand. Out of a bright light stepped an elderly couple - a tall man and a short older lady.

"Oh, Philip, how are you darling?" the lady asked. But I didn't recognise her.

"Oh, I'm all right, you know," I replied.

"Well, lad, about this bungalow," said the man. "Mother and I want Kath to have it."

"It's impossible," I answered. "We haven't got the money and I don't want it anyway!"

"Leave everything to us, lad. We'll sort everything out," said the man, ignoring my words.

At that stage the leafy man manoeuvred me away from the gate. The old couple waved, the lady smiling and the man just sort of looking at me from one side. I awoke the following day and as always with anything like that I went straight to see my mother.

"What do you make of it?" I asked.

"I don't know, Philip. I've not received any message for you, but your description of the couple sounds exactly like your great-grandmother and great-uncle, Dick, who lived in Darlaston. You'll just have to see what develops."

I drove over to Darlaston churchyard that afternoon with my daughter, Nadine, and just seemed to walk to a fallen headstone. We turned it over and it was my great-grandmother's grave. What could I do? I went home and told Kath the whole story, which she found very interesting. She knew me well enough to know that psychic messages or a dream like the one I'd had were not to be laughed at or ignored, but on this occasion she couldn't see any meaning to it. To be honest, neither could I!

7

The next day we got up as normal and I collected the mail from the letter box at the end of the hallway. One letter, a brown envelope, was obviously from an official source. I tore it open expecting a tax reminder or something of a similar nature but it wasn't. Some years earlier I had suffered an injury whilst at work that had kept me off work for quite some time. I had also been for a medical, which I had quite forgotten about. The letter read thus:

"Dear Sir,

We are instructed by our clients to offer you the sum of three thousand six hundred pounds, to be paid to you in compensation for an injury received ..."

with the date of the accident I had suffered included.

I handed the letter to Kath and told her, "I think you had better go and put a deposit on that bungalow!"

We made the move and to be honest I have never regretted it. I also spent a little money on repairing my great-grandmother and great-uncle's graves at Darlaston.

Life was really good for the next two years and then I was hit with a bombshell - my mother passed away. But I was to be warned and this helped me.

Firstly, one day when I was talking to my mother she told me she'd had some wonderful news from her main guides. When I was a little boy she had asked, pleaded really, to stay on the earth plane until I was old enough to look after myself. But when my daughter Nadine was born, she said she had asked once more if she could stay in this world and see her grow into a young lady. Mom adored Nadine, but by now we also had a little boy who was 18 months old at the time. Mom told me excitedly, "I know it's wrong, Philip, but I asked the guides if I could stay just a few more years and see Paul grow to become a teenager. I know it's wrong, and I have had more than my time here," [remember, she had been ill most of her life] "but they've told me I can stay until 1987, so Paul will be twelve." Somehow she didn't realise what she was saying - it was in fact 1987 then.

I didn't contradict her; something told me not to. I just went home and thought about what she had said that day. Later that year she fell very ill and was taken into hospital and then sent home still very poorly. Suddenly and quite unexpectedly she seemed to improve and the family, especially Kath, felt she was on the mend. Perhaps I did too, but later that week I had another dream and the leafy man was there again. This time I met a man I had not known on the earth plane but immediately recognised as my mother's father - my grandfather Will.

"Philip," he said, "it is time for your mother to come over to this side, and you're going to have to take care of all the arrangements on your side."

That was all he said. Quite to the point really, but then that was the way he had been in the body. Mom had often described him in that way. The next morning I awoke desperately upset. Shaking my wife I told her what I had dreamt.

"Phil, Phil," she said soothingly, "calm down, it was only a dream. Your mom is so much better now. It's just a reaction, it's just a dream."

I wanted to accept her logical explanation as she put it to me but I felt uneasy as I got up, dressed and went to work that day. Towards lunchtime I received a telephone message to go immediately to my parents' house in Willenhall. I didn't rush over or panic; a steadying effect suddenly came over me, but I knew my mother had left this world. I arrived at their home some ten minutes later. Dad was in a terrible state and motioned me towards the bedroom as best he could. I picked up mom's hand and kissed her forehead, "I love you, mom, I always will and I'll see you again." A voice in my head answered, "I love you too, son." And then she was gone. Mom had always told me that this was her last time on the earth plane, and who could blame her if this life had been anything to judge by. She was now progressing to a higher plane. That was her intention and I am sure she has.

The next 18 months seemed to fly by. I was now writing books, giving lectures and talks, and more and more my life seemed to be guided towards developing my mediumistic ability and learning about psychic matters. I did the odd radio and television spot and found I enjoyed the broadcasting side of things very much. One of the presenters of BBC Radio at the Pebble Mill studios, Birmingham, was Jenny Wilkes. She liked my work, especially the astrology, and asked me if I would like to give the astrology spot a try for a couple of weeks starting with a three-minute slot. Well, to say it proved popular was an understatement. I stayed with the BBC for the next three years doing a half-hour spot every Sunday afternoon and still return regularly as a guest medium, psychic and adviser on just about anything to do with the paranormal.

I have also written major features for Sunday newspapers and conducted on-the-air psychic experiments for the BBC. One example we called 'The Psychic Spiral' and joined forces with the Midlands' own Sunday newspaper, *The Sunday Mercury*, and well over half a million people took part. Some saw visions; spoons bent; watches and clocks started; others said they were healed of long-standing major illnesses. Perhaps as a top psychic and medium I had finally arrived.

Right now much of my life revolves around writing books and passing on wisdom and helping people as best I can. I have also been asked by my guide, MacDonald, whom strangely enough I only hear and yet has been seen by my wife, and another guide, Marian, to offer you their words as I am the medium they have chosen to work through in this world, but they always emphasise to me that it is up to you whether you listen or not. The choice always, as in any decision in any of your lives, remains firmly with you.

This introduction has told you a little bit about some of the stories you will read of in more depth as you go through my book and, of course, much more of my life and experiences are laid before you. If it helps you and you learn from it, nothing will please me more. If you think it is the work of an imaginative author or weaver of words, so be it. As with all things, in each and every one of our own lives, one way or another we are all eventually guided by the Light!

Telling It My Way
Extracts from a talk given at a large hall in the Midlands by Philip Solomon, who started with a very quiet audience and left the stage to thunderous applause!

Good evening, ladies and gentlemen. It's very nice to see you all here this evening. You know, some of you seem a bit surprised as you look up at me. I mean, what did you expect to see? Did you expect to see me flying round the hall on a broomstick? Or with wings or something? Because I'm not like that you know, really I'm not. I'm just the same as you, honestly I am! And I can tell you this much, if there is anything evil up here, or down there in the crowd, or anything spooky, you'd better clear the gangways, because I'll be the first one out of the building. [*Great laughter rings out*]. But seriously, it's lovely to be here tonight and to talk to you all.

To be quite honest, I feel that I ought to be down there with you really, because so much of my life has been spent in the Midlands and my great -grandfather actually came from this town. He was a miner in the local pits, and my grandfather and father also worked in this area and I have spent a lot of my time in the area as well, so I feel that I have come home tonight, so to speak - and I hope that you'll try to feel the same way about me by the time you go home this evening.

You know, ladies and gentlemen, I'm going to tell you something now that might surprise you. I doubt if there is a single person in this room who hasn't had a psychic experience or, at the very least, hasn't got a family member who has a strange story or tale to tell, so to speak. And that's not unusual at all, because the psychic world is for real and tonight I would like to tell you about some of my own adventures and the fascinating world that lies beyond.

I always retained an open mind, but little by little through my extensive investigations I finally became convinced that there could be communication between the living and the so-called dead who have simply moved on into a different vibratory level of eternal life.

I'll tell you something else that might surprise you. Many psychics get a lot of hassle from traditional religions. I never have. I've never had any hassle like that at all, and I'll tell you something else that might surprise you - I went to a church school (a very strict one at that) but I was never deeply religious until I learned this truth that seemed to be passed on from another world from guides and advisers. Actually, that really brought home to me the meaning of someone like Jesus's mission in this world; the reality of God; the oneness of all; a respect of all the world's great religions and the purpose for which we live.

I believe we are all one and each of us is part of our Creator and the understanding of the psychic world has made me a better person, certainly more spiritual, if you like. But the truth, as I'm learning to know it, transcends the boundaries of all religions; it is universal. This leads me to making a statement of what this is really all about and that is that you, yes you, will live forever! So for me, reincarnation becomes the name of the game! This concept of reincarnation is not new, you know, it's ancient, and let's remember that it is embraced by two-thirds of the world's people already, and according to my information was accepted as a matter of fact by many early religious groups - including St Augustine - until the second counsel of Constantinople in the sixth century condemned the teachings because it seemed easier to control the masses if they believed they had but one lifetime in which to behave before facing the so-called Day of Judgement.

Even today there are many good spiritual people who do believe, if you talk to them privately, that they have lived before. How many of you out there have experienced déjà vu? Come on, stick your hands in the air and be honest about it. Living several lives to me seems to be the only fair explanation for the unfairness of life.

Can we really accept that a loving God allows one soul to be born to wonderful, caring, loving parents but allows another to be born to uncaring, selfish, perhaps even those that can only be described as evil parents? It just doesn't make sense - not unless you have a belief that you will live several lives and your turn will come, so to speak!

How can you justify when a little baby is born absolutely perfect in every way in both body and mind while another little child comes into this life, blind, maimed, disabled? No one will ever be able to convince me that God wishes that to be so. God is love and God would not wish that on a little child. No, I believe that individuals must choose to be born into a situation of hardship or disability to learn and to develop, maybe to understand others and maybe in their next life it is their destiny to be wonderful teachers and helpers of people who suffer the same disability that afflicts them. Maybe some have been cruel to others, similar in situation to what they are in this life and need to experience, to learn and progress; that is also to be considered. Because I can tell you this much, friends, there is not one of us in this room tonight who is without sin, is there? And not one of us really who could throw the first stone at another either - well is there? Think about it. You see, it makes sense doesn't it?

Perhaps the people we call unfortunates, are actually the courageous ones in this life and have chosen to clear their spiritual slates faster than the rest of us!

My guides very clearly stress that we have to understand this concept of Karma if we are to recognise the true meaning of our earthly lives and prepare to get ready for the massive planetary and earthly changes that I believe are about to come about by the end of the century - but I don't think that is something that we should see as being the end, for I do believe there will be the emergence of a golden age of peace and understanding and love within the twenty-first century.

But here again let me say to you that I do not believe in death - we will all live forever. I believe that this body you have now of course dies, but you then simply change your energy frequencies and move on to another existence on a different vibration level, and if those on earth were to learn how to tune into that vibration I'm sure that you would see these other lives existing and living! You know, it always seems strange to me - I can't understand why people laugh at the old lady who says that she is talking to her husband who has been dead for 12 months. "What a loony!" some may say, but maybe she has lived on this earth for 90 years and learned a lot. She has progressed and probably knows far more than someone who is 23 or 24 and thinks they know it all! How do you know that she is not tuned in and talking to that person? Because they certainly do exist on another level; another frequency; and maybe she has tuned into them. Think about it, ladies and gentlemen, and consider the possibility with an open mind.

Remember, when you are listening to your radios, there are hundreds of stations to choose from and if you move the dial you can get one of those stations. For example, you could be listening to local BBC radio and might hear me every Sunday, then you move the dial a fraction and you've got Radio One - you have got something on another frequency, move it again and you get nothing. The secret is that you know how to adjust and tune in to those stations. Think about it the next time you laugh at old Bessy; maybe she is more developed than you are and it's as simple as that really - it's all a matter of tuning in!

The ultimate aim for all of us must be to live loving, helpful lives, then eventually we will be, in my opinion, returned to our Creator - the same

Creator who sent down our soul for our first life, our second life, our third life - and, of course, the last life that we must live to progress enough to reach oneness. We all have free will and if we misuse and abuse that gift then, yes, we have many lives and many lessons to live and learn from. But we are so lucky in my opinion, at the time that we live in now, for we are at the beginning of the so-called New Age about to hatch - the Age of Aquarius if you like - that's what a lot of people call it isn't it - The Age of Aquarius? And astrologically speaking, of course, that's basically what it is - an age of love and understanding. Those of us who are here to experience it in this lifetime, or perhaps the next, will indeed be lucky and blessed.

So let me thank you for being you and thank you for being wonderful, and I am really hoping tonight that I have stirred some questions in your mind. I don't ask you to believe; all I ask you to do is think about it and just consider it for yourself. But, you know, occasionally I believe that our past lives come to the surface anyway. I wonder how many of you out there in the audience have found yourself inexplicably drawn towards certain people or, should I say, souls. Why is it that the loving husband, or the loving wife and mother, walk away from a marriage or relationship and just go with someone else? Honestly, I'm not making an excuse for people, and for those of you that have been hurt by an experience like that it's hard to accept, I know, but honestly sometimes I just don't think we can help ourselves. If they come from a past life and someone is there who you knew in your past life, you can't help it. Have you not heard people say: "I just couldn't help myself!" Think about it; it can apply to some break-ups you know.

Some of you out there must know of a child who has the most brilliant artistic ability in music, or a foreign language, or for drawing, painting, sketching, and both the parents are absolutely hopeless at such things - could they be actually drawing on subconscious memories or prior knowledge from another life? It is possible isn't it? Do you have a love of a particular food, especially you ladies when pregnant and carrying new life? A yearning to visit certain faraway lands and then when you get there you know for sure that you have been there before? Come on, you all know what I'm on about don't you? I know that you do because it's the truth! These are indicators of lives we have once lived before. Ladies who remember that whiff of a long-forgotten perfume or fragrance will know what I mean.

And children; you know children are so psychic and they often speak of earlier lives when they are very small. But, of course, parents tell them to stop telling stories or making up tall tales don't they? Indeed, they may actually be telling the truth! When you dream, this may also be a clue to your long buried past. Psychics are people who develop what they call clear vision and use the inner eye or, more appropriately expressed, the third eye, to see past lives. In fact, for many it is an integral part of the art and work they do.

Let's look at meditation. This is really just a process that links us with the heart of goodness, or your God, if you like. Right or wrong are not always clear choices unless deeply contemplated, and meditation can be the answer. But if you harm someone else, either by thought, action or by not doing what you should, then meditation would teach you that you harm yourself also. I believe that your spiritual growth progresses with every good thing that you do in life or say to help another, especially if you don't look for rewards for it and you leave it secret, so to speak! But it is important that we all realise that the earth's overall spiritual growth cannot be accomplished by one person alone. It has to be the total effort of the human race and it is up to me and every single one of you out there to help everybody else when they are in times of need or going through a rough passage.

But look, let me tell you a little story that my mother once told me. It's about a man that passed over and went to what he perceived to be his heaven. This man had been a good man in life, and in his view had done no wrong at all. He'd never stolen anything; never robbed anyone; never cheated anybody; worked hard in his life until he was 65 years of age and never had a day off work; went to church every Sunday; and was the first one to put his hand in his pocket to give a pound for charity. Well, he passed into the Spirit realms and woke up in what he perceived to be heaven and found himself in a country lane which he walked down, smiling happily. Halfway down that lane he met a real rough and ready, old farm labourer-type fellow.

Looking down his nose at him he said to this chap: "Which way to God, please?"

The farm labourer looked up at him and said, "Friend, the way lies within."

By now the man was getting a bit aggrieved and demanded that he be shown the way to God, the Judgement Seat, and so on.

"Look within, friend," said the farmhand again. "You'll have to judge yourself before you're able to join the Creator."

"But I've never done a wrong in my life," replied the man, now quite upset.

Whereupon the farmer, who was in fact an Old Soul, told the tale of his last earth life, which he'd thought had been pretty blameless as well, because he'd worked very hard all of that life and had actually served on earth as a lay preacher and had also worked very hard to help poor people in his farming community.

Once more the new arrival asked, "What can we possibly have done then that displeased God?"

"You still can't see it clearly can you?" commented the farmer. "We've both been too concerned with our own selves to stop and help those less lucky or fortunate than ourselves! Look in this pool over here and I'll show you something in the reflection."

The man did this and immediately saw a vision of his wife, who was still on earth, talking to that nosy Mrs Jones from next door.

"How you managing, love, since he's gone?" Mrs Jones asked.

The man's wife looked down for a second and then answered, "Well, you know, at times it wasn't easy to live with a saint, especially a self-ordained one!"

He was shocked to hear his wife talk about him like this but it made him realise that he had forced his own ideas of what was right (and righteousness, if you like) on others, whereas love and understanding would have probably served him much better. However, by now he had been taught the way of things by the farmer hadn't he?

Being really tired and having learned his lesson, the man held up his arms and said, "Okay, will you take me to the Judgement Seat now?"

The farmer looked at him, winked his eye and said, "Well face it, friend, you're already sitting on it! We all are, aren't we?"

A lot of you have probably come along tonight hoping perhaps to hear one or two of my little psychic snippets or messages from the other side.

Well I'll leave you with just one message tonight if I may, and I won't ask you to accept it or believe in it but just ask that you will think about it in your quieter moments: life is forever; listen to everything, listen to everyone, and try to gain knowledge to help you progress. Get into that meditation, learn some of the techniques; it could be so beneficial if you think that's right for you, because it is a very valuable tool with which to open your mind to an understanding of the reality of less perceived worlds and meaning outside the present world that you know of. We are all here on earth to do one thing and that is to learn. We have all been here before and many of us will have to return again and again, always confronting and challenging ourselves and learning to progress. In the end we do eradicate all our faults and achieve reunion with the Creator of all, which of course we are all a part of anyway. Do your very best always to seek the light and goodness and try to pass on to others all good things that you have learned. But, above all, prepare yourself and the earth for the New Times - a Golden Age that can belong to us all if we learn to think about things more spiritually and less materialistically.

Thank you very much, ladies and gentlemen, for listening to me tonight, and always remember: if you care and love enough, you can change anything! A goodnight to you all.

Chapter 1

The Circles in the Sand

A lot of people sit for many years in circles to develop their psychic or spiritual abilities, but I suppose, having the parents I did and being born into Spiritualism, much of my basic training had been done naturally as a little boy. I, like many others, however, decided in my twenties that I would go along and have a taster of what was on offer outside of my family. I was probably foolish to take that action because if I had asked my mother about the type of circle I was going to visit she would have definitely told me to keep well clear of it.

But I liked to do things my own way in those days and arranged to visit an address with a girl I knew at the time and went to this so-called circle of development. When we arrived the other people were already there and we were led into a small back room where seven or eight people were sitting on hard-backed chairs in a perfectly formed circle - man, woman, man, woman, etc. - and I was placed in one part of the circle and the girl I was with in another. They all seemed to be much older than us; some of them looked to be 70 or 80. Sitting down, I counted round and noticed that, including us, there were ten people altogether. One very high chair stood on its own and empty, so I asked the old lady sitting next to me who it was for.

"Shh!" she replied. "Relax yourself. That is the chair of the Great Lady, a very fine medium."

"Who?" I said.

"The Great Lady," she answered again. "The medium. She's in the other room and will join us shortly to give us her words of wisdom."

An old gentleman on the far side of the circle suddenly raised his hands and asked us all to sit very quietly and a door on the other side of the room opened and in walked a tall, dour-looking woman, clenching her hands and mumbling some words that I couldn't really catch. She sat in the chair and looked around the circle.

"My friends," she announced grandly, "you are very lucky this evening. The spirits are with me and I shall communicate their words to you via my wonderful clairvoyant gift."

One of the old gentlemen turned off the lights and we were in complete darkness, yet the moon shining through a small window made each and every one of our faces clearly visible. The medium, with great theatrical aplomb, grimaced, threw back her head, made a sound similar to belching and started to speak.

I tell you, friends, I have been brought up around the Spiritualist and psychic world all my life, but I had never seen anything like this and I didn't know whether to laugh or cry. I could see the girl who had come with me was a bit scared though.

The medium relaxed somewhat and spoke aloud, "Do not be afraid, especially you little children who are new to this religion." (I assumed she meant my friend and me, but I was 20 and certainly no child.)

She pointed to one of the old ladies to the left of me and said, "I have your husband, William, with me, my dear. He is showing me a parrot. It's name is Polly. Do you understand?"

The old lady replied, "Well, no, not really. My husband was named Tom actually, but we did have a budgie!"

"That's right," said the medium. "That is the connection. But did you not know that when your husband was a boy they called him Willie and that your budgie has now ascended to the higher life and taken on the form of a parrot? How wonderful this is for you, is it not?"

She then pointed to me, "Do you know you have a gift that you could develop, my son?"

I tried to answer her tactfully, "Well, we never stop developing really, do we?"

"Yes," she replied, "but your Uncle Alf wants you to get close to people who have the gift, those that can develop you as a medium and make you more understanding of the wonderful gifts that I have, for instance."

That was enough for me. I thanked her for the message and immediately closed myself down. After about 20 minutes, which seemed like an eternity, they finally closed the meeting and put on the lights and a man whom I presume was the medium's husband asked me and the girl I was with if we would like a cup of tea. I declined as I could see my friend was looking nervous. She hadn't enjoyed it at all and it had been a pretty awful experience for me too.

He also said at that stage, "We absolutely refuse money from anyone but, if you would like to make a donation, be assured it is always put to a good cause," and he promptly placed a five-pound note on a saucer.

The statement he was making to me was quite clear and, feeling rather embarrassed, I put my hand in my pocket, fiddled for some change and dropped it on the saucer. My friend did likewise and we left. Returning home that night I told my mother of my experience.

"Serves you right really, doesn't it?" she said. "She was no medium and that's not a proper circle. What you should be doing with your wonderful gifts is getting yourself down to one of the Spiritualist churches. You don't have to come to mine if you don't want to, but go to one and sit in a proper closed circle."

"Closed circle - what do you mean, mom?"

"Well, every church has various circles and many have what we call an open circle where anyone is invited and it is good as an introduction to developing your skills. The only trouble is they often have so many people go to them, perhaps 25 or 30, that the medium or experienced person teaching doesn't always have the time to get round everyone to help develop them or, in some cases be in control, and that can cause problems for someone with abilities like yours, son. What you really want to be looking towards is joining a good closed circle."

I heard mom's words but never really took much notice of them and went on developing myself by reading and learning of the work of people like Lyall Watson, Edgar Cayce, Sir George Trevelyan, Tom Lethbridge, and my mother's medium friends, like Gordon Higginson and Harry Edwards, the great Spiritualist healer, and almost anything else I could get my hands on from the necessary type of background. In honesty, that was probably the end of my circle work up until mom's passing to the higher life.

When my mother passed away in 1987, I suppose like many people who have just lost someone, the physical loss was very great. I knew she existed somewhere but I wanted someone else to tell me and give me a message and prove this to be fact. So I started to go to Wolverhampton Spiritualist Church. It would have been very easy to have gone to Darlaston where my mother had gone for 50 years, and Mary, my grandmother, who had gone there before that for many years as well and where I would be known and very welcome. But everyone also knew mom, and all the mediums that went there - well - let's face it, I would have been very sceptical of anything they told me. So I headed towards Wolverhampton Spiritualist Church, and like any other church it had its fair quota of people who were very nice, and those who had obvious psychic and mediumistic ability, those who thought they were mediumistic, those who thought they knew about the spiritual and psychic world, and a large congregation who just wanted proof and assurance that their loved ones still existed.

It was there that I met Dennis and Marsha Barnes, wonderfully caring people, whom I feel will remain friends of mine forever. I also met a very good medium called Sheila Green who used to take the circles there, and just out of interest I went along to the open circle, which was much as mom had described it really, a very large gathering of people with a little bit of ability but probably with more of an interest in Spiritualism generally. I went for about two or three weeks and Sheila and I just naturally became very good friends. She used to ask me to go along to help with the circle, rather than sit in it, which I did, and on occasions she used to bring out of the circle five or six people whom she felt needed bringing along and developing and I would take them into the back room for her. I've always had a lot of time for Sheila, and believe she is a first-class medium, and again, although we don't see so much of each other now, I feel we will always remain close friends.

My father by now was also a working medium taking the rostrum in local churches and on one occasion he actually worked with Sheila at the Heath Hotel at Bewdley, in a charity event to raise money for a little girl who was quite ill. Hundreds of people attended that meeting, and if my dad was the star of the show, Sheila wasn't far behind.

There were also two other people who regularly attended the church, and who operated on the committee, called Rona and Dennis Sheldon.

Rona was a novice medium, just starting to do work on the rostrum and she seemed to have a very promising work schedule ahead of her. They asked me if I would join the closed circle and every week about five or six of us would meet in the back room. This was to prove a more successful way of developing my gifts but, without wishing to appear big-headed, I was so far in front of everyone else there that it usually ended up with me going round the small circle showing them how good I was. However, this wasn't what I wanted so I moved away from it.

All the time I was at that church, with the exception of Marsha, Dennis and Sheila, one or another seemed to be pushing me towards getting up on the rostrum and becoming a working medium, but that wasn't what I wanted to do either, nor did I feel it was right for me, and by now my guides, MacDonald and Marian, were influencing me away from it too. I still went to the meetings but I would have people coming up to me from the congregation asking my advice about various things and I would tell them what I felt was correct for them and fortunately, or unfortunately as the case may be, the evidence and snippets I gave them were so accurate that at times it would make what had been given from the rostrum seem silly and trivial. I think it sometimes offended 'the powers that be' who ran the little church and poor old Sheila was given the task of telling me that I shouldn't give messages, as they called them, to people in the church. I didn't lose my temper with her because I realised it was the others that had made her say it, but I thought to myself, "God Almighty, these people must have no spirituality at all! It doesn't matter whether it comes from the rostrum or the floor, if you get it for someone you've got to give it!" I think a lot of the problems lay with two or three people who held power at the church and who had very little psychic or mediumistic ability, let alone spirituality, but they were very good people in their efforts to help others develop their skills, so perhaps they should be credited for that.

I had pretty well decided that I was going to move on from Wolverhampton Spiritualist Church, as it wasn't the work I wanted to do, but one matter particularly brought it to a head and again it was probably my good friend Sheila who did it, although I am sure she didn't realise it at the time. I was asked to a meeting to take a vote on who the new committee would be and about 30 of us were deciding on who would take on the various roles when Sheila, who was the resident medium, said a few words about the progress that a lot of people had made in the circles, etc. She then turned to me and, in front of everyone who really had any power in that church, pointed to me and said, "We have in our presence Philip, someone who is very special. He has such wonderful abilities that we all really should try to get him to progress and go forward in whichever way he really chooses for himself. This is a young man with a very special gift."

I could hear the tuts and groans, and there and then I decided that that was it, it was time for me to move on from this church and to pastures new. I didn't hold a grudge and I didn't blame the people with whom I had my experiences, but it was clear that they would never be broad-minded enough to take the spiritual and psychic world further forward in the way I would wish. But what was I going to do? How could I achieve it?

That very evening driving home from the meeting it seemed that MacDonald, a wily, canny old Scotsman was to step in and take his chance to guide me to his way of things.

"It's time, lad," he said somewhere in my mind, "to start thinking about making your own circles, about teaching others all the wonderful things that you have learned and pass on the gifts your mother gave to you when she gave birth to you; to tell people of the things told to you by many others. Remember how you were born as Gordon Higginson predicted you would be? The way Mrs Grainger came into your life and taught you real Spiritualism when just a young boy? [You, the readers, will hear of her later on in the book]. All the old ones that you met through your mother who passed on their wisdom? It doesn't have to be in a church. Pass it on in your own natural way and know that I, and your other helpers, will always be there to help you speak the words that will be required."

Over the next few years this seemed to happen naturally in my life. I was asked to give talks to people, I became the honorary president of an organisation called the Ghost Hunters' Club of Great Britain, an opportunity to explain to people who were interested in ghosts that there was more to it than howling ghouls and spectres and that it might be spirits that abound and people might be trying to get in contact with them and they may have a role to fulfil in life. I was also approached by

Birmingham Local Authority's Adult Education department to see if I would conduct evening classes in psychic awareness by just looking at the subject of the psychic world and explaining to people how they could be more involved and achieve things through their own inner abilities.

I accepted and started off with a half-hour lecture at Great Barr School in Birmingham. Over a period of two years I have found that I am lecturing every night for Birmingham Local Authority and that when we enrol the classes at the beginning of the year the 20 places available to a class are filled within about 15 minutes and as I sit at my desk taking students' particulars, prospective students are before me three and four deep clamouring to hear what I have to say.

While teaching there, I met John Routley, one of my students who would excel and become known as 'the Birmingham Medium', and a man who started to support me in 2006 in my theatre demonstrations. I often sing a couple of songs at these shows, Elvis Presley and Billy Fury-type songs, and John always insists that it is more than just me singing their songs; I am so like these artists in voice and presentation, they overshadow me. But this is something you will read of in more depth further on in the book.

It is amazing really because a lot of things link back to my experiences with the Spiritualist Church. Two elderly Birmingham ladies readily spring to mind, Doris and Winnie, who had been sitting in the type of circles I have told you about for 20 to 30 years and had never really become developed psychically or got anything else from them for that matter. They came along to my psychic awareness class for beginners and I taught them various simple things about meditation, going into the quietness, learning to focus upon a singular object, bringing oneself into the calm, and proper psychic protection. I also taught them to use pendulums, a bit of dowsing, and then moved on gently towards the psychic and spiritual realms, and within 12 months those ladies were developing very quickly into very good mediums. Indeed, in 18 months they were happily going round passing on little psychic snippets that were readily and perfectly accepted by the rest of the class. Here were two ladies who had probably spent 27 years trying at the Spiritualist Church, and within 18 months with me were as good as a lot of people standing on the rostrums claiming they were something special. I don't take credit for that myself because I believe they always had the ability, it just needed to be brought out properly in them. I still take these classes, but they are based at Cannock College now, and I do very much enjoy doing them. Financially, it doesn't seem very worthwhile, but to me it is very worthwhile to see those people progress and achieve something from their own abilities, and it pleases me greatly when I see that my two ladies are now international mediums and working abroad too.

However, I must say that I do have many dear friends in Spiritualism and there are some very good circles. Not everyone has the same experiences that I have had. Indeed, perhaps my experiences are special. We have to be taken through life's journey in a way that puts us on the right path for us and I feel that is what my experiences have amounted to. Many other young people go through the Spiritualist system and become good at doing what they want to do basically to help others. It does seem, however, that many people who hold power in these churches seem to emphasise that it takes years and years of development before one can get up on the rostrum and pass on messages from Tom, Dick and Harry, Auntie Jean or Aunt Sarah, and that their way is the only way to achieve spiritual enlightenment.

I disagree on both points. Firstly, if you have very good natural ability (although we are all psychic and can eventually achieve this) you can very quickly learn to portray your art professionally to others; and secondly, if you don't think the Spiritualist Church is right for you, and so long as what you do is for the good of yourself and others, then I don't think there is any wrong at all in finding another way to spirituality and understanding for yourself and others. Like I did, go for it in your own way! Or be guided by your own inner guides, for they are always there and their words will come to you. If what you want to do is beneficial then there will always be words of wisdom.

The same applies to healing. Many people will tell you that to be a healer you have to be trained, again usually through the NSU movement, who will advise you that you need to get a diploma, a piece of paper that tells people you can heal. It also allows you to wear a nice white jacket and wave your hands in the air or perhaps draw your hands back and forth close to the area that someone tells you they feel pain. Let me say here and now that there is nothing wrong with that, but there are other ways to heal. I believe that some of the greatest healers in my lifetime have been people who can make you laugh. I believe not enough laughter is the problem in many people's lives including illnesses. If you are happy and you can laugh then I feel you can cure yourself in many ways, and if as an individual you feel you have goodness about you that you can pass on to others then do it. If you are a person that so wishes to heal but you would like to take courses that lead you to certificates, diplomas and the ability to be professionally recognised as a spiritual healer, then so be it, but what I would suggest is that you also learn a lot more about the psychic world generally and if someone is not very well, just wish them well, say a prayer for them if you like, ask for whatever energy and power you have to spare to be sent out and towards them to bring about balance and to make them feel better, and it does work.

People ask me if I am a healer and whom I have healed. There are one or two celebrities I have worked with and when I was at the BBC I would perhaps receive 10 to 20 letters a week from people asking if I could heal them, if I could make them better, or if I could make their lives more happy. I always wrote back whenever I could telling them I would send my thoughts out towards them and it was amazing how many letters I got back saying things such as they didn't know what I had done but they were feeling so much better. You, too, can do that.

One thing I will say, though, is that it is always important to protect yourself before doing any work and this is not very difficult to do really. Simply say a little prayer to what you perceive to be goodness or godly - it doesn't matter whether you are Catholic, Protestant, Hindu or Jew, pray to whatever you perceive to be God. If you are an Atheist, send out your thoughts to what you perceive to be good in the world - I'm sure you can find something - and ask that you are protected. You may ask me why you need to do this and I will put this point to you. Everything has a good and bad side; we have our own free will to choose what we tune into. I would advise you never to tune into what you perceive to be bad for obvious reasons; it could put you out of balance and could even be dangerous for you in some ways.

Looking at it through the eyes of a Spiritualist, if someone wasn't very nice in this life, perhaps even described as evil, when they pass over to the higher life it is my belief that they would be much the same as they were in this life and wouldn't have just suddenly changed - it may take many years before they become a better person, and if you were to contact them it is likely they still wouldn't be very nice to know or to communicate with.

I will tell you of another method that in my experience will always keep you safe called the 'spacesuit technique'. Basically, all you have to do before commencing any spiritual or psychic work is to visualise yourself wearing a spacesuit and a fishbowl-type helmet on your head with an opening front: just close it up and know you are protected from any outside forces. I know it sounds strange but it works well. To some it might be known as closing down the aura, but it is basically sending out the thought pattern of protecting yourself that counts, and if you use either this method or a prayer to something that is godly or good it is my experience that you will always find yourself to be quite safe.

These days, I am so busy lecturing, writing major features for newspapers and magazines, doing radio and television work and, of course, writing books similar to the one you are reading, that I rarely have time to sit in another person's circle or to go along to development classes in one form or another, which is unfortunate really and I am going to try to make the time in the future because I feel we all benefit from that sort of experience, but I shall make certain they are good ones I attend and that I do progress through them, and that is good advice for anyone wanting to progress in a proper way.

Don't just listen to what one person or group says. Go out and learn for yourself. Be like me and get lots of experiences. That's how I got to the stage I am at today, recognised as a top Spiritualist medium and teacher. Don't bury your head like the ostrich does because you can't or won't understand something. Insist on asking questions and receiving answers and knowledge, or you may end up getting lost forever in the circles in the sand, hence the name of this chapter!

You may also be interested in Reiki healing. I am a Reiki Master Healer teacher and this type of healing uses what we call 'universal healing' to benefit others. There again, I also still practise traditional spiritual healing. I find somewhere between the two is perhaps right for me, and you may find there are other methods of healing that work for you and others perfectly too. You just have to search and find your own pathway in these things.

Chapter 2
Experiences Equal Wisdom

Some personal experiences that have occurred for me in life may seem strange and unusual but I am sure many have had similar experiences but blank them from their mind or are too scared to accept that there is significance in them and that, indeed, experiences equal wisdom.

My wife, Kath, once bought me the most beautiful crucifix and chain you could imagine and I absolutely loved it as I looked at it in its beautiful velvet box, which is not surprising as three of my possessions at that time had been another silver crucifix and chain, a large gold cross and a pendant of the healing hands, so you would expect me to be attuned and in balance with this lovely present she had bought for me. But no! There were problems as soon as I put it upon my neck. I felt a strange tingling sensation and found it uncomfortable to wear, but not wishing to upset my wife I continued to wear it for a few days.

Unfortunately, Kath found me most disagreeable and, indeed, aggressive. Could the crucifix be the key? Surely not. Such a wonderful symbol of love, peace and the forgiveness of the world's sins. There was only one thing to do and that was to ask my mother what she felt about it. Taking the object in her hand she told me not all was well with the gold in this object. Psychometry led her to believe that the gold had been taken originally from an ancient tribe (perhaps stolen would be a better choice of word) and bad vibrations had remained within its base metal format, although it had been made up into many different objects in many different times over and over again.

She took it to the Spiritualist church at Darlaston of which she was president, had it blessed, prayed over it and generally put it to rights. But on this occasion it was not to be the answer, because whenever I wore it an amazing thing would happen. Unseen forces would remove it from my neck and return it to the dressing table drawer in my bedroom. On one occasion it actually vanished from my neck in the presence of my wife and other family members. I rushed upstairs and there it was in the drawer of my cupboard! Mother once more looked into its background and decided it had been removed by my grandmother who was in Spirit. She felt it had a bad balance to me apparently. That was good enough for me - it was a present and I wouldn't part with it, but I put it away and left it as I had been guided. Strangely, my wife told me that she once secretly meditated with the crucifix and she had a very frightening experience of seeing a man who scared her greatly. In recent years I have spoken of this matter with the guide MacDonald, who leads me to understand that I may keep this gold but not wear it, until it eventually finds a way to be returned to its original owners in another faraway continent. Many people such as myself, psychic consultants and the like, speak of good and bad gold and I have given you a personal experience to prove that point.

On a personal level, these days I never buy or accept presents in precious metals, or diamonds or similar stones, until I am absolutely sure it is suitable or, indeed, good or bad for me as an individual and this can be easily ascertained for others also. Before you buy something new at the high street jewellers, take it in your hand and see how you feel. If you have a tingling sensation or you don't feel at one with it, perhaps it's best to look for something else.

Coincidences are also strange matters in my life and I know anyone who is reading, or has read other books by me, will be in no doubt of the closeness that was felt between myself and my mother and of a similar bond that exists between myself and my wife. When we were both little children, I about nine and she about seven, one bright sunny day we both saw what we now describe as a UFO. I had seen a huge glowing orange ball, similar to the moon, that travelled at a great speed across the sky and seemed to draw my attention as if it were almost hypnotising me by its light. When I first met my wife many years later, I told her the story of this great glowing ball and, to my amazement, she told me she had seen exactly the same vision but in her case her mother had been with her at the time and had also seen it. Now, to the best of my knowledge and, indeed, following a lot of research it seems that no one else actually saw this vision. Could this have been a premonition or psychic link of our future together? I believe it could have been; in fact, I would say that I know it was, for this is the information that is passed to me by my guides. However, I should be very fair and say to you that my wife does not share my absolute belief in the spirit world. She is very sceptical of most things psychic and spiritual until they are proven to be positively true. Perhaps she is my balance in the psychic pathways and work as a medium that I feel it is my job to follow in this lifetime. However, I believe that I am a very lucky psychic in as much as I am one of those people who seem to be a facilitator for psychic phenomena or strange occurrences to happen while others are within my presence and, indeed, sometimes seem to cause experiences for them to occur. This is also very important when you can call on these people to prove that what you state is fact and to prove the existence of the psychic world.

Let me give you an example. I was once with a very dear friend of mine, Leslie, a very intelligent young man. We were both about 16 and were walking home from our place of work. We both worked for the Decca Record Company, which had manufacturing premises in Wolverhampton at that time. As we walked over a nearby bridge I noticed right in front of us what can only be described as a tiny green man. Yes, I know it sounds incredible but that's what it was, a tiny green man or a goblin. I pointed to him and Les just stared.

"Are you seeing what I'm seeing?" said he.

We looked at each other and then watched the little man cross over the bridge and move down into some fields that were alongside the bridge and then just vanish. At that particular time I had no real interest in aliens, UFOs or anything else of that nature and, although certainly psychically developed, had never brought anything at all of that nature onto my vibration, although I must say he seemed perfectly amicable and friendly, smiling as he passed by.

Not only was Les a great friend of mine but he was also one of the greatest jokers you could ever wish to meet and was frequently known to play tricks, and in that context I demanded to know how he had set up this practical joke! But the fact is he hadn't and to this day, many years on, he is as flabbergasted by what we saw as I am. I suppose I cannot say for sure that it wasn't someone dressed up, perhaps a midget from a travelling fair, but equally I don't think that I'll ever be able to say that it wasn't a goblin or perhaps an alien. What I do know for sure is that it was a totally unexplainable experience.

Another psychic experience that happened to me with friends present was when I was about 17 or 18. Robert and Tony Kennard and three other friends were present at my house when mom and I were having a bit of a disagreement. I wanted to go to a party that would continue all night and come home the next day. My mother, with dad's support, made it perfectly clear that if I wasn't home by 11 o'clock that night, I would be in trouble. I was extremely tense, and angry that in front of my friends I was being told that I was still a child, that I couldn't stay out all night and that I would have to do as my parents said. Mother, in particular, was most insistent that on this occasion I would do as I was bid. At that time we had a television set that was kept in the corner, a black and white set similar to what most families would have had at that time and, as with most families, ornaments and vases were placed upon it. Ours was no exception. Upon the television set, mom had put a pretty blue and white vase in which she had placed some tulips.

Once more I asked mother if I could go to the party and just as quickly she told me that I could not go. I turned and looked away in disappointment and anger and focused my attention upon the vase. Immediately I did this, one of the tulips rose up, floated across the room and fell at my feet. I shall never know why and, in fact, it was a subject my mother would never discuss, but she immediately turned round and said I could go to the party but I had better be pretty sure I behaved myself! I did go and I did behave myself but I had very little peace from Robert and Tony all night, who wanted to know how I had performed the trick that convinced my mother that I should be allowed to go to the party. The thing is, though, it wasn't a trick and I don't know how I did it myself. I can only imagine that my pent-up energy, anger and psychic ability had raised that flower and convinced mom that it was important to me. Perhaps I had reached a stage in my life where I needed and should have had a bit of freedom.

As I have got older and more developed as a psychic consultant, I have come to believe and have the understanding that this is the same type of energy force that people such as my friend Uri Geller and the like use to bend spoons by intensifying and focusing the psychic energies on a singular object and, well, anything can happen.

But these were not always pleasant and amusing experiences for my friends. I well remember Robert Kennard, who had been my best friend for most of my life, staying at my home one night. At this time we lived over a shop in Willenhall in the West Midlands which was owned and managed by my parents. They sold all sorts of goods really, ranging from fishing tackle to household goods, cigarettes, haberdashery; just about everything you could imagine. It was a real old curiosity shop, borrowing the words of Dickens, and, in fact, the whole building was strange to say the least! The time I am talking about was Christmas 1969, and that year all the little girls had been asking their parents for large Spanish dolls, very beautiful dolls that came in their own individual large boxes. Mom and dad had sold so many of them, and taken orders for those to be collected for Christmas, that the upstairs rooms had been stocked with them, my bedroom in particular. In fact, one side of the room was filled with them.

Anyway, Bob and I had been to a dance in Wolverhampton that evening. We came home quite tired and went straight to bed and I fell straight asleep, that was until Bob woke me up with a sharp elbow in my back.

"Phil," he said, "stop being silly. You're making stupid noises and opening boxes and trying to scare me and you've got something with a child's voice on it. I'm telling you, Phil, you're making me angry. Don't carry on with it!"

"I don't know what you're talking about," I replied, "and you're making me very angry for waking me up. Stop being so daft!" And I went back to sleep.

Once again Bob woke me up and this time he was furious, insisting that I had better pack it in, to use his words without the expletives! At that stage the boxes of dolls literally fell over and flew across the room, crashing against the opposite wall, and a large vase that my mother kept in my room also floated in the air then smashed against the wall. Bob jumped out of bed, switched on the light and insisted on talking for the rest of the night - he was very, very scared. It was unfortunate really because we had stayed at each other's homes for about five years and, indeed, I continued to stay at Bob's home, but he never ever stayed at our house again after that night and the experience with the dolls!

As usual in these matters, I asked mom to explain things and she did very matter-of-factly. Apparently, the guide she dealt with mostly to communicate to the other world was a little girl who was often about the building and she had a very great love of these dolls we had stored in the rooms. Apparently mom had communicated with her guide and what had basically happened was that she, as any other little girl might do, was looking at the dolls, peeping if you like, and hadn't intended to frighten Bob at all. She'd been startled and panicked herself.

In all honesty, that sort of thing wouldn't frighten me anyway because I know there would be some sort of answer for it and mom's explanation to me was perfectly acceptable. I passed on this information to Bob but I think it scared him even more.

"Oh yeah," he said, "and what about the vase that floated in the air and then smashed against the wall, mate? Kids don't throw great big vases!"

Oh well, as I said, these experiences for others aren't always as pleasant as I wish they could be!

I did have a frightening experience myself once, but that was when I was about 19 or 20. By then mom and dad had moved to a house in Kelvin Road, Walsall. This house, apparently, had once belonged to a gentleman and his daughter. His daughter had left the house some years before but he had stayed until his passing over, at which point the house moved into the tenancy of my parents. I slept in the back bedroom and early one morning I awoke and sensed a pair of hands belonging to a man around my neck, strangling me. It was a terrible experience and only really stopped when I managed to scream out and my father ran into the room to see what was wrong with me.

It was just a dream, you may say, but later that night our neighbour, Mrs Olive Taylor, the mother of two friends of mine, Carl and Stuart, unnerved me somewhat, because she told me that the man had been a very strict father with his daughter who used to sleep in the bedroom that was now my room. Whether something of his former self had remained in the house and walked into the bedroom finding a very handsome young man (even though I say so myself) in the bed where his young daughter would have lain, I could never be sure, but I was only a developing psychic at that time and insisted that exorcism or whatever would be the appropriate move before I stayed in there again. Mom laughed at me really but went through some sort of ritual that satisfied me and I never had any more problems, until I met my wife to be, Kathleen, who stayed over at our house at weekends and used to sleep in my room. My mother would make up a bed for me on the settee downstairs, but to be honest Kath was so frightened by the cold, scary feeling she described that the minute she could she would shoot downstairs and we would spend most of the night talking.

Years later when I left home and had children of my own, sometimes my aunt would stay with my mother and father and, as it was only a two-bedroom house (and yes, I suppose my aunt had heard the stories of the back room), she slept with my mom and my dad slept just once in the back room! Now, as I have said, my dad is also psychic and a very good medium and he claimed his sleep was disturbed. He said he woke up and, looking in the mirror, saw the face of a man whom he could only describe as glaring! As far as I know the room was never used by members of my family after that, despite the fact that it is now completely clear of any untoward vibrations.

But really most of my experiences and coincidences have been very pleasant and, indeed, lucky. Right from when I was a little boy I was fascinated by sport and particularly enjoyed horse racing. Mom's family had been farming and horse people and perhaps an interest in that sort of thing was in my blood. My dad's father had also been a very accomplished amateur jockey and horse rider and dad was also good with horses. Although under age, I must admit that I did love to have a bet - nothing desperately out of order, usually a two-bob double. However, on one occasion I really did want to win; it wasn't just the fun of having a bet, I really felt I needed to win. Now I must say that I have always been told you cannot use your psychic abilities to do things like that, but on this one occasion I did try and it has to be said I was successful and I won some money.

I had been reading about the racing that day and visualised the two horses winning in two races, and to this day I still remember them. It must have been about 1964. One horse was called Cash, at 50-1, and I just knew that it would win the race and, indeed, it did win the big hurdle race that day. I also saw a white horse, Richard of Bordeaux, winning the Mackeson Gold Cup and, indeed, it won at 20-1. What a double - 50-1 and

20-1! Dad collected my winnings and the only real disappointment I had was that I was robbed by the bookies through some obscure rule they had that limited the payout and I never did get all my money. In all truthfulness and honesty, I have never been able to visualise anything like that since, not for myself at least. I do remember coming home once from a holiday in North Wales in about 1964 or 1965, however, and having an exhilarating feeling come over me that I would be getting something, but I didn't quite know how. Strange as it may seem, as we drove into Wolverhampton that day there were pictures of my dad up on the newsboards, and when we got back to our house the little Indian boy who lived next door, Kalwant, was waiting to tell my dad that a man with a big camera had been waiting for him all day and that his father had given the reporter a photograph they had of my dad to publish. Kalwant then thrust a piece of paper into my dad's hand asking him to telephone the *Express & Star* newspaper in Wolverhampton as soon as possible. He did and was duly told he had won £1,000 on Mark the Ball. That was a lot of money in those days - I suppose it would be like winning £30,000 or £40,000 today. And I did get something very special - dad bought a new bike for me, a new car for himself and also took us on a far better holiday than the one we had just been on, together with my Auntie Bertha, Uncle Ivor and cousin Glynn.

Other strange occurrences, of course, have also happened to me in life. Perhaps one of the more unusual ones was when Kath and I were first married and we had our daughter Nadine. At the time we were living with my mother and father and we had very little money to spare. Although my parents were very kind to us, kept us really, and did their best by us, Kath was becoming very unhappy - it was not like having our own home and she was becoming increasingly depressed and disillusioned. We tried very hard to buy or rent a house or to get accommodation of some sort so that we could have somewhere of our own with our little girl and be a family, but it was 1974 and I suppose we were like many other young couples with a baby in that year - accommodation of any sort, bought, rented or otherwise, was very hard to come by. However, my mother told Kath that in March of that year we would get our own house and I had little doubt that if mom said it, we would get it, although at the time Kath perhaps didn't really believe it!

Out of the blue our first home fell right into our hands really. We used to go out on a Saturday night with most of my parents' family to a little club called St Mary', which was situated in Willenhall town centre, and two of the people who went there were very good friends, Frank and Minnie Starkey. One evening they came and sat by my mom and they were talking to her about general things, the way you do in that type of club, when Frank happened to tell her that they were leaving their little terraced house in Gipsy Lane, Willenhall, to move into a new council flat. Frank and Minnie were a lovely couple, but unfortunately she had been blind for many years and the house in Gipsy Lane was very run down and not really suitable for Minnie in her condition. To cut a long story short, they were moving into their new flat the following month and they told my mom that the owner was going to rent out the house out as she didn't want to sell.

What an amazing situation. We asked Frank if he would speak to the owner and see if it would be possible for Kath and myself to rent the house, which he did, and when we went down to see the owner she said we could have the house if we wanted it, but perhaps we should go and have a look at it first. It was a bit of a shock when we did go and see it. It was more than a little old-fashioned to say the least and plaster was falling from the ceilings. It was damp everywhere, there was no inside toilet and it was in such a state of disrepair that it was understandable that Frank and Minnie had been provided with a council flat - it was bordering on being uninhabitable. But we liked it and the rent was a very nominal sum, so we took it on. At this time Kath and I were getting on much better with her parents than before we were married and after a short time we borrowed the money off them to buy the house at a very affordable price because of the state it was in.

The first job that had to be done really, having a baby in the house, was to provide a bathroom at the rear of the building and perhaps the sensible way to have gone about things would have been to apply for a grant. I'm sure we would have got one but, to be quite honest, we just didn't have the money. I was working at the local locksmiths down the road, Josiah Parkes, a job I hated, and would go into work at 8 o'clock in the morning and work until 9 o'clock most nights, seven days a week, just to get the money to pay our loan back and survive, and believe it or not we paid for that house in just twelve months.

Therefore next, in my wisdom, and with a little bit of odd-jobbing help from family members, I decided to demolish the rear of the property and build a bathroom on the back myself. Having never done any building work in my life, this was to prove a fatal mistake. Demolishing the building was very easy! Kath's father came and took down the chimney and we smashed the roof and quickly reduced to rubble what had formerly been a brewhouse and washing area. Only one problem remained: I now needed to transform that area into a bathroom and kitchen, and I had never laid a brick in my life. In all honesty, I really didn't know where to start and I realised how foolish I had been.

In the last 18 months or so, I had not had much time for the spiritual and psychic side of life. I had been much more interested in the material side and getting on with improving life for my wife and daughter. My grandfather, Arthur, who had done some building work in years gone by, came to the house and was very willing to help me try to get the bathroom built, but he was 76 and I knew he had a bad heart and wasn't very well so I couldn't accept his help. I didn't really have anyone else to turn to. My dad helped me as best he could, but he was more of a mechanical engineer than a builder!

I didn't know what to do, so one night I just went to the bedroom and quietly sat down and sent my thoughts out to the spirit world, to other-worldliness, a psychic connection, whatever you want to call it, and asked that I would be given help. I don't know how my prayers were answered, all I know is that they were, and that I was given the help I needed. Over the next six weeks I set about building that bathroom. I did all the brickwork; I did all the carpentry; I repaired the roof; I even plastered the walls. From having no experience whatsoever, I just know that in some way my hands were guided and helped and things were put in order and as they should be. Now I didn't do a very brilliant job of it, I'll be the first to admit that, but it lasted us for the next five years and we made a healthy profit when we sold the house. Perhaps I knew there and then that if ever I needed help in my life in any way I could always gain it by simply sending out my thoughts to the spirit world. This has always proved to be so even to this day, although I never try to do it except when I am really desperate.

There have been other occasions when I have really needed help and received it. I was once taking my IWO Diploma in Welfare Work and had to take an exam in psychology. Arriving at the examination centre, in all honesty I knew I couldn't, and didn't deserve to, pass the exam because I hadn't done the work, but I needed to pass that exam because it equated to more money and progression in my career. As the other students tore into their examination papers, I very quietly went into an attuned state and asked for help. A calmness came over me, I picked up my pen and filled in the paper - and passed with distinction. I don't think that I really cheated, though, because ever since then I have had a great understanding of psychology and I think the wisdom was put into my mind as I passed the information down the pen and onto the paper, and it has remained there. That seems to have been the way throughout my life. Whenever I have really needed guidance, help or positive assistance, the spirit world or the psychic world has always been there to help me and I do believe they always will.

People also ask me if psychics are warned of danger and if I have had experiences of that type of thing in my own life. I believe you are put here on this earth to experience and to gain wisdom and to grow, and that we live many lives before we make progression to be with our Maker, but I also believe there are times when we are protected and kept safe by those that love us, perhaps those that have moved into the spirit world on the first plane. I remember once, in about 1972, I had been out with my girlfriend, Kath, and after taking her back home we had a disagreement with her mother over something fairly trivial. I left her house in Wolverhampton to drive back to my own home in Walsall and, driving very fast as I turned into a place called Bentley Lane, I suddenly heard hands banging on the window of door on my side of the car. I reduced my speed, pulled over and got out, but nothing was to be seen. However, I heard a voice that I perceived to be that of my grandmother, even though I had only known her for about 18 months when I was a very little boy. It seemed she was saying that something was going to get me or something was going to hurt me - I can't really say for sure - but what I do know for sure is that I drove very steadily down the lane after that and when I reached the bottom I found that a large lorry had careered onto the other side of the road. I have to be honest and say that due to the speed I was travelling before I was slowed down by those hands I would almost certainly have hit that lorry and would probably have been badly or fatally injured. I do believe that evening my grandmother (my mother's mother) had protected me from something that would certainly have hurt me. Of course I have had other similar experiences, we all have, but we perhaps don't think about them in a psychic context until we see how they have changed our life or protected us.

As I have said previously, my wife is one of those people who has to have things proven to her. If she saw what she believed to be a ghost or spirit, she wouldn't just accept it as a natural occurrence, she would look for what had caused it. However, she had an experience one day at Warwick Castle, which I can assure you is a place where ghosts and spirits walk, in which she saw something she just couldn't explain. For some reason she was drawn to walking towards an older part of the castle that generally is not so attractive or visited by the general public, when she saw some steps that led up to a tower. She felt compelled to walk up the steps and, looking up at the tower, she could see the head and shoulders of a young woman in a cornflower blue dress and wimple gazing out through the window of the tower. This stopped Kath in her tracks and she watched as the woman seemed to fade into the brickwork at the back of the room. By the time Kath was able to tell me about the experience, the lady in question had vanished completely. The tower and surrounding buildings were derelict and there were notices everywhere warning people not to enter the area as it was dangerous, but she insisted that we looked around closely to make sure that no one was in the tower. There was absolutely no way into the building, and even Kath had to admit that day that without a shadow of a doubt she had seen what could only be described as a ghost.

A very unusual occurrence, perhaps a time-slip situation, also happened to Kath and my son in 1991. The three of us had been on holiday to Tenby in Wales and had driven out on a trip to Pembroke to visit the castle there. On the way they had noticed a sign for Lamphey Bishops Palace, and Kath and Paul wanted to visit it. I wasn't having any of it and carried on to our agreed destination. On the way back that evening it was starting to get a little dark, but Paul (a great fan of castles and old buildings), with the support of his mother, was adamant he wanted to visit Lamphey

Bishops Palace. I don't know why, but for some reason I had a great feeling of foreboding and really did not want to go to the place that day. But they were insistent.

On parking the car, we discovered that it was closed but it was still possible to go in and look around.

"Please, let's not go in," I said. "I have a really bad feeling about going into this place!"

"Don't be ridiculous," Kath replied, and off Paul went with his mother following on and, yes, me dragging behind at a fair distance!

After Kath and Paul had walked round the grounds, they climbed up some rather rickety steps.

Paul suddenly looked over and pointed to an archway. "Hey, mom, look at the garden and all those beautiful flowers in there. Come on, let's go in."

Paul started back down the steps and ran towards the archway. When Kath looked at the archway, however, all she could see was a huge wooden door which was tightly closed. Alarm bells were ringing in her head and she screamed at Paul not to go in. Giving chase, she caught him by the collar just as he was about to step through what he later described as an open door and a beautiful garden behind it. When they looked again, however, the huge open wooden doorway that Paul had seen and the tightly shut door that Kath had seen had disappeared and all that was there was a large archway that had obviously been bricked up for many years!

If Kath hadn't caught Paul that day, would our son have slipped through a time space of some sort and into another world? An even more chilling thought: if he had gone in, would he have been able to walk back through the doorway from the garden that he could see? Who can say, but I can assure you Kath quickly found me and agreed that we should get away from there as quickly as possible. We have visited this place at other times and with all the other visitors there it has seemed quite pleasant, but my feeling about it that day was that it was not a good place for me and mine to be at that particular time.

Checking out the history of Lamphey Bishops Palace, it seems that the medieval bishops of St Davids, who had great power and status, had built the palace for themselves as a magnificent retreat away from the work and pressures of Church and State. Research suggests that they had everything on hand to entertain them: fish ponds, lovely parklands, fruit orchards and yes, you've probably guessed it, flower and vegetable gardens!

I started this particular chapter by talking about coincidences and here, perhaps, is the greatest coincidence that has ever happened to me and those I really care about in my life, which would certainly include my dear mother, Elsie, and my wife, Kath. About six months after I first met Kath I asked her if she would like me to buy her something special and she said straight away that if I were to buy her anything she really cared for it would be an eternity ring. I was surprised but at the same time very pleased to hear her say it and we agreed that that weekend we would go into Walsall, Wolverhampton, Bilston, etc., and see if we could find one that would be suitable or that she liked. I don't like to complain, but she walked me round for three days looking in almost every jewellery shop that you could imagine, never really sure of one that she liked. Some weren't quite right, some didn't have the right stone, some didn't feel right, I could understand that, but she seemed to reject everything she looked at, until finally we went into one jewellery shop where they brought out a tray with the eternity ring she liked. She pointed at it and said that without a shadow of doubt it was the ring she wanted. Very relieved I paid the assistant, Kath put on the ring and that night she came home to show it to my mother.

Mother said it was very pretty but asked what had made her pick that one in particular. Kath answered that she didn't know, it just seemed to be the only ring she really liked. Mom looked amazed and told us to hold on a minute. She went upstairs to her jewellery box and took out an eternity ring she had bought two or three years earlier, basically just because she really liked it. She brought it downstairs and, yes, you've guessed it, haven't you, readers? It was exactly the same ring that Kath had chosen out of all the hundreds she had looked at. My mom really loved Kath and, indeed, Kath really loved my mom, so perhaps it was no wonder they would pick the same ring, but it really was a most amazing coincidence.

Chapter 3
Further Experiences

It is hard to talk about your experiences, real-life, psychic or imaginary, especially those that happened as a child, because that is a time when you are never really sure of anything. There are lots of lessons to be learned, lots of new things to be sampled, perhaps a time when the adult to come within you is being moulded, even though at the time you probably don't realise it. Childhood for me in many ways was very mixed; it could be a very happy time or very sad, never much in between. I really loved living in the country in Wales and by the seaside. Even then I think it brought about and charged my psychic abilities, whereas when I came back home to the West Midlands, usually during the winter, I didn't really like it and in fact at times I hated it, but a lot of that really had to do with school - I was never very happy at school and my son, Paul, seems to have been much the same. Of course, like any other father, I had to tell him it was the best time of his life and stress how important it is to get an education, but it is hard to give a convincing argument sometimes because I never found it very worthwhile myself, and Paul, who is now 22, often reminds me that I didn't always tell him the truth in such matters!

Wales seemed a good time to be with my parents, especially my mother with whom I was able to spend a lot of time and I really enjoyed that. Then dad would come down at the weekend and I would have him there too. My parents were business people. My mother was always running some shop or pursuing some business venture and it was the same with my father, who was a rock 'n' roll promoter, augmenting his efforts to break into show business by sometimes being a lorry driver, chauffeur, etc. I never saw a lot of my parents as a child really, and mom was often ill and seemed to be in hospital much of the time. When she was at home, though, I remember she did have some fascinating friends, especially those colleagues of hers that were interested in Spiritualism and the spirit world generally.

One in particular, Mrs Grainger (I always called her Auntie Millie), was a real character. She was a very upper-class sort of lady who always carried a walking stick and gave off a strange aura. She was very wise and very kind in some ways, and yet she also seemed stern and at times could frighten me. She always promised she would buy me a pony and asked if I would like dapple grey or chestnut brown, but she never did. Yes, I can hear Mrs Grainger now. One thing she did have was an amazing understanding and knowledge of the religion of Spiritualism. Equally well, she could almost quote the Bible word for word from beginning to end; a very religious lady. If Charles Dickens were alive today, surely a book would be penned about Mrs Grainger!

What I remember the most about her were the times when she would sit at the great table in the front room with my mother and I would creep to the door to listen to what they were saying - foolish really, as I knew the things they talked about would scare me, and they did! It is hard to remember all the things they discussed and it seems very funny when I stop and think back in my life, but I do remember Mrs Grainger would talk about her husband, Albert (who was dead), visiting her in the middle of the night and speaking to her through a large trumpet, advising her how she should go forward in her life. Then mom would tell her about her experiences and the way she communicated with those in the other world and how she had helped and guided such and such a person by making contact with those they had loved and lost.

By now, Mrs Grainger's son, Peter, was seriously involved with another family friend, Sheila Aston, and they were engaged to be married. To me Sheila was always a very nice person and when I was about five or six she looked after me in the evenings while my mother and father were out at business or running dances and in fact that was how they first met her. She was only about 13 and was fascinated by the rock 'n' roll movement and she used to sell the mineral water and crisps in the refreshment area at the venues. When she wasn't doing that, poor old Sheila would get lumbered with looking after me, and I could be a right handful, that's for sure! But I did really like Sheila, who I'm sure wouldn't mind me describing her as a typical little Black Country wench - outgoing, bubbly and full of life. I always saw her more like a big sister than the girl who looked after me and I still see her that way to this day. Peter and Sheila did marry but what an unlikely couple they were. Peter is completely different - a very reserved, educated, deep-thinking man, of whom I am also very fond.

When we were living in the Midlands and I was about eight years old we moved to a great, rambling house called Wellington Villa - not a particularly happy time for me as a boy, I might add. It was huge with numerous rooms, including several bedrooms and a massive bathroom. It also had very large grounds and its own stables. I also have to tell you that without a shadow of a doubt it was haunted by several ghosts.

I was nine when my mother had to go into hospital for about six weeks. Dad was very busy and there were many occasions when I had to spend time alone in that house, and it could be scary! I was a natural medium for sure even then, and could see people and things that would frighten me. I will tell you of one of many incidents just to give you an idea of what it was like.

One day I was in one of the large rooms at the rear of the house on my own when I heard knocking and banging in the hallway. No one else was there except me and we didn't have a telephone at the time, so I felt quite scared. What I did have was an Alsatian dog called Bronco that I'd had from a puppy and I loved him very much indeed. We spent so much time together he almost became human. So I hugged him and we quietly moved towards the door. I have no doubt that animals sense the other world and are very psychic, although some people would disagree with me. I opened the door, looked down the hall and saw a man who must have been about six feet three inches tall, dressed completely in black and wearing a very large top hat. I froze as I looked at him and he turned towards me and seemed to blink. Could this have been a time-slip experience? Was he seeing a little boy from the future as I was seeing a man from the past? That was just one experience typical of the kinds of things that happened to me there. It was a very strange house, Wellington Villa.

I also remember once seeing what I would now describe as a footman in the stables and, again, as I looked at him it seemed as though he had seen me too, although no words passed between us. The gardens were also strange. They were very large and I used to see a lot of children there, dressed in old-fashioned clothes. I used to speak to them and two that come to mind in particular are a little boy called David and a little girl called Matilda who were very friendly.

I have spoken earlier about coincidences and that leads me back to the tall man who stood in the doorway. Many, many years later whilst I was researching for books similar to the one I am writing now, I came upon the work of a very famous Black Country psychic called Theophillus Dunn and found a drawing of this man who had lived in Netherton around 1866. Amazingly, he was the absolute image of the man I had seen at Wellington Villa. I can't claim that it was him, but I would be very interested to find out if he had at some time visited Wellington Villa. If he did I am sure that was the man I saw. It was also at that house that I seemed to become more aware of my guides and those that would help me in life, so perhaps this is a good time to tell you about them.

Once on my bedroom wall, at a time when I was not very well, I saw what I can only describe as looking like two copper plates. On one of them the face of a Chinese man seemed to form and, on the other, the face of a Red Indian man. When I first saw them I was very scared, so much so that I actually lost my voice for a while, and yet gradually I came to understand that they weren't there to frighten me but to watch over me. Of course these are very progressed guides and even as a little boy I seemed able to communicate with them on a telepathic level. They seemed to be telling me that all of us have a spirit guide or guides to show us the way to follow our tasks and go forward to do our work on this earth. They also communicated to me that, although sometimes I was unhappy and had to go through hard times that I couldn't understand, this is what I had agreed to do before I lived this life. It seems strange, but I remember once being really frightened by what I realise now was also one of my guides or helpers. It was a Red Indian wearing a bear's head, but all I really focused on when I visualised him was the head of the bear and it really scared me. I realise now that he was probably a man with a lot of wisdom, especially in the healing ways, and I don't find it at all scary now when I think back on it.

I would think it must be difficult being a spirit guide because I suppose most people don't give guides the time or space to communicate and tune in, even though we all have them. Of course, as I have progressed and become a developed Spiritualist medium I have come to understand that meditation is probably the most important and best method to use to make contact with your guides. For those of you reading my book, you should realise that making that sort of contact for the first time should be done alongside someone with a lot of experience who knows what they are doing and can take you along the pathways gently and at just the right time in your life.

Round about this time I also became aware of two of the guides who very much help me in my writing and who channel most of the work towards me that I present to you in the various books I write - MacDonald and Marian, although those are not necessarily their exact names but that's as close to the pronunciation as I can get. Every one of you has similar guides to Marian and MacDonald as well, although many of you probably haven't learned to communicate with them in the way I have or the way they would choose to communicate with you.

Making communication with your guides can be important. It certainly has been in my life. In fact, I can't really imagine living my life as I do without having this contact available and I speak to my guides on a fairly regular basis, at any time of the day or night and about all sorts of things, not just the serious things that I feel need channelling to the world to those that want to listen. Marian tells me our guides are drawn to us by pure love, they are not forced to work with us, so to speak, and that they have been contacted and drawn alongside us in several different lives and that in this life, as in all the others, they want to help us to achieve all we can and to grow spiritually as much as possible.

I think sometimes you have to be careful how you explain that to people because they often think this means the guide influences you or gets you to do what they want. That is not so. They are called guides because that is precisely what they do - they try to guide you to make decisions about you and where you are going to go in life, and I think that with a lot of meditation and psychic development some of us do reach a stage where we can communicate and ask for help and the guide then becomes almost like a constant friend that you can talk to in times of need. It seems to me, from my work as a psychic consultant and adviser to others, that a lot of people never actually know their Spirit guides exist or communicate with them at all, and thus live this life and pass over to another state totally unaware of the wonderful friendship they could have attuned to if they had wished to learn. Having said that, I think things are changing today. I find now that five days out of seven I am lecturing at different classes, teaching people about psychic awareness, how to be more spiritual and, hopefully, moving them towards awareness and understanding of themselves and a closeness with their guides so they may communicate and be guided from a higher level. So to all my students who are reading this book, and no doubt there are many thousands of you, you will know why I spend such a lot of time on the meditation techniques, because that is how you can basically get to where you want to be and achieve what you want to achieve.

I have several guides, as does everyone, but one will be very special and is often referred to as the Door Keeper. He or she has been with you from the very moment you took life in your particular body. I have told you how I have been helped to pass examinations and do building work I knew nothing about, and I think it is fair to say I am making a reasonable case to prove that receiving help from somewhere certainly happens! Many guides come into our lives at different times, basically because they care about what we are doing and wish to help us progress in this life we are living. I don't greatly publicise my work as a healer, but there are plenty of people I have helped who know that I do this work and have the healing ways. Those of you who are healers or are training to be healers will find that you learn at an accelerated rate and that you get help from otherworldliness and your guides, I am quite sure of that fact. When I heal I am quite aware of the guide, or spirit guide if you like, Dr Chang, drawing close to me and helping me to help other people. In terms of the books I have written in the last few years I will openly admit that I am helped by MacDonald, a huge Scotsman who has far more literary ability than I am ever likely to have and yet never had the chance to present the written word in his time on earth. I feel greatly honoured to present books to the world with his assistance and guidance, and that is the key - he guides and helps me.

I believe much of my life and the way I live it has been planned for me by my guides. Perhaps that is one of the reasons I felt I never really fitted in with the traditional religions of our country nor Spiritualism at one time, but I was to return quite quickly and do the work there as a medium and healer. A great medium, Gordon Higginson, said that I would and so did my mother and they were right. Indeed, it seems that in Spiritualism today there are a lot of people who are now coming round to seeing things in a similar way to me, but I don't find that all mediums and Spiritualists have the same views on how churches should operate and perhaps that variety is progressive in some ways.

Modern Spiritualism is claimed by those that believe in it to be a religion because they say it moves towards the understanding of the spiritual and physical laws of nature which are, in fairness, the laws of God, and they communicate with the spirits of the dead to give proof of survival to those who have lost loved ones. In the Spiritualist Church there are also those who heal, and a Spiritualist minister can both marry people and perform funeral services. Today, with the certificate and diploma courses, mediums have to reach a very high standard in order to be able to perform, especially on the NSU rostrums. I would never wish to offend anyone, however it is my belief that a white jacket and waving your hands in the air will never make you a healer, and neither will a certificate or diploma make you a medium. Some people are born to be mediums; others develop the gift over many years. I believe a certificate or diploma are of secondary importance to those efforts and one thing that has always seemed completely wrong to me is how everyone in the church used to focus on getting information from just the mediums or speakers who took to the rostrum, because I learned I could get knowledge from many sources and, most importantly, from within myself through meditation and study, and you can too.

Today thousands of people visit Spiritualist mediums and Spiritualist churches to be guided and comforted in grief but, in my experience at least, they were very rarely told that they could get it for themselves and that their own guides would give them the best individual guidance. In my opinion and experience this was never properly explained to those who came that were new to Spiritualism and had a fresh interest in other-worldliness. But there you are, I could be wrong, and I often am - that's the way of learning in life - but my guides rarely are!

Let me give you a very personal example of the way my guides helped me at a time when I really couldn't cope. I was only a little boy of about 10 or 11 and, yes, I mean a little boy! I thought I was grown up but at that age we're not, are we? Many of us remain innocent in many ways really. Anyway, one particular day around this time of my life was to prove very hard for me to bear.

One morning my father told me that mom was very ill and might not survive a big operation she would be having that morning, but I had to go to school and be brave as no one could look after me and he didn't want me to stay at home on my own. I didn't want to go to school that day but dad was very worried himself and I didn't want to make matters any worse than they already were. That morning we lined up for assembly and, as the youngest children in the school sat on the front row, all eyes were upon us. We had to listen to Mr Edge, the headmaster, going on about the meaning of life and why we should be good boys and girls, honour our parents and be respectful of our elders, especially our teachers. But my mother was in hospital that morning, maybe dying, and that was the only thought in my mind so his words just went above my head. I know it is hard for adults to understand, perhaps it is for me looking back, but one of the things that really worried me apart from mom was that I would break down and cry in front of my friends. Children being children, I knew they would be cruel, would not understand and would torment and jibe me. It was unbearably difficult for me and I felt a tear upon my cheek as the children broke out into the chorus of 'All Things Bright and Beautiful'; I knew I was going to cry. Then suddenly I felt a presence on either side of me, helping me, holding both my hands and keeping me upright. I can't say who it was that drew close to me that day, because I don't really know whether it was Marian or MacDonald or perhaps other guides and I was certainly too young to tune into them, but I knew from that day onwards that I would never be alone and would always be helped in times of trouble.

Writing this book, I have to be honest and say that I wasn't that sensitive as a child and I wouldn't want you to think I was. In fact I had developed into a very tough kid in a lot of ways and would rarely walk away from a fight. I was also very good at football, boxing and other such sports. One day one of the very toughest boys in the whole of the school was beating up one of my cousins. I told him to stop it, so he immediately turned his attention to me and said, "Okay then, mate, I'll see you after school and give you some of this too!"

I wasn't a kid to back down and answered him straight away, "All right, I'll see you on the playing fields."

I knew in my heart that a beating was highly likely to be coming my way but it wasn't to be. After school the two of us walked towards the playing fields with a very large group of other lads, cheering us on - kids can be cruel and bloodthirsty at times, can't they? It may sound silly, but just before we reached our destination somehow I felt a strange presence coming over me, overshadowing is perhaps the best way to describe it, and felt like a great boxer or fighter. I have no wish to go into detail about the fight or gloat in any way except to say I won easily and very quickly, and if you read this book at any time, Billy, I'm sorry mate - maybe it wasn't a very fair match really!

Let me return to that sad day in assembly. I didn't cry then and rarely have since. I wish I could sometimes. I respect any man who can show his emotions in that way and I believe it is a powerful way to release the tensions from within for some. There have been people in my life who haven't understood me in that way. "If you're so sensitive, how come you never show your emotions?" Even my own father has said on one or two occasions that nothing seems to get to me and that it seems I don't care. You're wrong, dad, it's just that I am well protected, looked after and guided, but the tears do remain within.

Chapter 4
Ummo and the Road
to Nowhere

As a top psychic consultant, Spiritualist medium, long-term feature writer for *Psychic News* and a person who has been involved in the psychic world all my life in one way or another, I have been told about and have investigated many stories of UFO mysteries and all sorts of alleged encounters of alien visitations. I have travelled pretty well all around the world, but one strange fact is that wherever you go people are always interested in two things: the psychic world and the existence of UFOs and aliens.

Spain, in particular, is one of my favourite countries and it was there that I was told of a very interesting group of people. Interesting? I should say amazing actually! These people call themselves Ummo and have been corresponding by email, letters or telephone calls throughout the Spanish countryside for the last 40 years. They claim they landed on planet Earth in the French countryside in 1950 and are here with the specific task of helping all the inhabitants of Earth. They call themselves Ummo because this is what they claim is the name of the planet they came from. All the correspondence sent by these people is not signed but is finished with a thumbprint at the bottom of the document, together with a curious symbol that looks like three horizontal lines across one vertical line. Some of my friends in Spain assure me that in 1967 - yes, as far back as 1967 - a group of people were invited to prepare themselves for a set date, 1st June, at a restaurant called the Santa Monica close to Madrid where evidence and proof would be given of the Ummo's existence. I am led to believe that the group attended and a craft that the group could only describe as a flying saucer landed, on the underside of which the Ummo symbol could clearly be seen. Many good witnesses claim that the UFO passed over several times and performed aerial tricks, I suppose in much the same way that our own Red Arrows perform today. It is claimed that some of the witnesses actually took photographs of the UFO before it suddenly zoomed away at great speed. Unfortunately, no one since, myself included, has been able to find out anything more about the Ummo and three questions must remain unanswered: did those people at the restaurant see a real UFO? Did they see what could be described as aliens? Or could it have been a David Copperfield-type illusion? I can't be any more sure than you, but it is a fascinating story.

What I do know is that late in 1972 Kath, who was my girlfriend at that time, and I had what can only be described as a very strange experience. It was about 7 o'clock on an autumn evening in October and we were travelling in my Morris 1100 car towards the village of Bridgnorth, which is about 18 miles from Wolverhampton. It was a cold, crisp evening, but really fairly clear. The roads were pretty good and the weather didn't seem at all bad. We left Bridgnorth and carried on towards another village called Ludlow in Shropshire, intending to visit The Downs Hotel and Restaurant, a place frequented by many young people from the Midlands as it had a very good discotheque, but as we left Bridgnorth we found ourselves on a road that we couldn't recognise. This didn't concern me unduly at the time, as many of my family came from Shropshire and I pretty well knew my way in and out of the little villages that surrounded Bridgnorth, so we just drove on.

It was about 8 o'clock at night when suddenly we drove into what I can only describe as a really dense fog and yet we could see quite clearly right ahead of us. The fog seemed to be on either side of the car, hugging into the wings. I know it sounds odd but it is the only way I can describe it. Something else alarmed us at this time: the road we were travelling on seemed to be getting quite narrow, but we thought we must just have strayed off the beaten track. After continuing for about another quarter of a mile, I told Kath that we were definitely lost but not to worry because I would take the next right turn and drive back in the direction we had come - all those different lanes eventually led back one way or another to

Bridgnorth. Almost immediately that right turn became available and I took it, but unfortunately the fog seemed to thicken even more. I also realised that this right turn had taken me onto a very steep hill, although that was something of an understatement because as we progressed along the road it seemed as though we were driving up the side of a mountain. The lane we were in had also closed right into the sides of the car and we couldn't see a thing except what appeared to be very large bushes or something similar on either side.

I changed the car from top gear, to third gear, to second gear and found that my vehicle could barely climb the hill. By now Kath was very scared and was starting to panic. Really you had to be in the car to experience the sensation of the steepness of that hill and I was scared myself, I must admit, very scared. Although I turned to Kath and told her to be quiet as I knew what I was doing, really I didn't feel in control at all and the hill seemed just to get steeper and steeper. It felt as though we had travelled a very long way and by this time I had had to force the car into first gear but still it was struggling to climb; even in first gear we did not seem to be able to reach what surely must be the approaching summit.

At that moment an influence seemed to come over me. Was it Spirit? Was it my psychic intuition? Perhaps it was just common sense telling me that my little Morris 1100 car could climb no more! I don't know which of those things really drove me to it but at that stage I slammed hard on the footbrake and pulled on the handbrake at the same time. The car stopped but, terrifyingly, because the hill was so steep it immediately started to slip slowly backwards.

Kath was terrified. She looked at me and grabbed my arm saying, "My God, what's going to happen to us?"

"All I can do now, love, is reverse the car down the hill and get us out of here," I answered.

"You can't, Phil, there's no way you can do it! We'll be killed!" she screamed.

"Stop it, Kath," I said.

If I say so myself she is a spirited girl and not much upsets her, but she put her hands to her face, put her head on my shoulder and just prayed that I would pull it off. Very tentatively, I slowly released the handbrake and the car immediately started to hurtle backwards at great speed, so very gently I applied pressure on and off the footbrake hoping to halt its speed, but in all honesty I could barely control the vehicle. I also used the handbrake to slow down its travel and I think I placed the car into reverse gear, but I am not sure of that fact. Amazingly, after what seemed like a few seconds, two things happened: the road seemed to widen and the thick fog seemed to clear into a light mist.

After what seemed an eternity, but must only have been seconds, we found ourselves back at the bottom of the hill. However, again something very strange had happened: it now wasn't the very narrow little lane we had driven up but seemed to be a reasonably major road. In all honesty we didn't spend very much time looking at it as for some reason I was very scared, which isn't usually my way with these sorts of things. Normally, I would get out, have a look at the situation and investigate all the possibilities. On this occasion, however, I pushed that little car as fast as it would go away from the area and then pulled over at the side of the road. I don't think I have ever felt so afraid; my heart felt as though it would burst in my chest it was beating so fast. Kath was very pale and she also was very, very scared. We hugged each other and I said shakily, "I think we nearly went into eternity there. That really was close to the end of the road for us, but at least we would have been together." She agreed and kissed me.

We really didn't want to go anywhere else that night. We were too shocked by the experience and just wanted to go home. Kath looked at her watch and exclaimed that it was 11 o'clock, her deadline for getting home. If she didn't get back in time, World War III would be likely to erupt, as her mother could be very difficult about arriving home late. So we got ourselves together and headed back to Wolverhampton, which I suppose was about 22 miles from where we were - if I knew where we were! Strangely, though, I immediately saw a sign for Bridgnorth and headed towards it. Within seconds we were in Bridgnorth town. I drove up another steep hill - nothing like the previous one, I might add - called the Hermitage, which leads out of Bridgnorth and back towards Wolverhampton. The car didn't seem overheated or damaged in any way and got us back to our starting point. I dropped Kath off at her home and drove back to my own house in Walsall, but I couldn't sleep that night for thinking about what had happened to us.

The next morning I went back to Kath's house to pick her up and asked her what she thought had happened. She couldn't explain it either except that it was very frightening, but what we both decided there and then was that we must go straight back, retrace our tracks, and perhaps park the car and walk up the hill to see what we had experienced, so we drove back to Bridgnorth, then towards Ludlow, following the route we had taken the night before to try to find the hill.

Unfortunately, we just couldn't find it. There was no trace of it at all, and many, many times over the last 30 years we have tried very carefully and with numerous enquiries to find the hill that led to nowhere, but to this day we have never been able to locate it. I can't claim that it was anything supernatural or, indeed, that it was a psychic experience, because we didn't finish the journey to the hill's summit to find out what was or wasn't waiting for us there and, in all honesty, that is one journey on which I have not regretted reaching the ultimate destination! Obviously, I was quite young then and have told this story many times since to friends, colleagues and others who have a great interest in or knowledge of the supernatural or psychic world. Could it have been an encounter with some unseen force? I'm sure I don't know.

One thing that is very strange and unexplainable relates to the time we spent on the hill. At the very outside it must have been about 8.30 when we started the trip up, then we spent perhaps 15 to 20 minutes climbing, which would have taken us to around 8.50/9.00, and we certainly came back down that hill in reverse very quickly, in not more than three or four minutes, so let's be liberal and say by the time we reached the bottom again it was 9.15. I then drove back down the main road for perhaps five to ten minutes before parking up, which means that when Kath looked at her watch it should have been around 9.30, but it was actually 11.00.

Somewhere along the line we had lost at least an hour and a half that we could never explain; it is as though we had been somewhere else for that period. All the both of us know for sure is that we had been on the road to nowhere! Could this have been some kind of UFO encounter, or perhaps even an alien abduction? All I can say is that as yet I have not been given the answer as to how or why it happened.

Chapter 5
There's No Place Like Home

When Kath and I got married, we spent the first 12 months living with my mother and father, and then we had our first home, a little terraced house in Gipsy Lane in Willenhall. It was a very strange house in many ways really, but always incredibly lucky for us. We always had enough to eat and a good life, never a tremendous amount of money, but whatever I turned my hand to seemed to be a success. The strangest thing about that house when we moved in was birthdays. I was born on 23rd July and this birth date was shared with the man who lived there before me, Frank Starkey, the man who lived next door, Harry Butler (Ivy, his wife, was to prove to be quite a character and a good friend to us) and apparently the man who lived in our house before Frank - quite an amazing coincidence.

About the time we moved in I got a new job for an organisation called the Crypt Organisation in Wolverhampton. The man who set up this organisation was called Geoff Parsons, a wonderful person who always tried to help those that really needed it, and if anyone was worthy of receiving the title 'Sir' then in my opinion Geoff Parsons deserved it for the work he did with the underprivileged and those that others didn't really care about.

It was a very difficult job really, as I had gone in there to work with lads who had a history of mental illness or had suffered from stressful lives, and it was my job to reintroduce them to working life again, but it was a job I really enjoyed. Also, the Crypt had a great many lads and lasses that came from a West Indian background and were members of a group called the Rastafarian religion. They had a youth club there which many of these young people would frequent, and quite often I had to work there and help out advising people generally. When I first started working with these black lads it was very difficult to relate to them. I was a white face which to them just represented authority and someone who was out to get them or at least get them into trouble. But, as the weeks and months went by, I gradually made friends with a lot of them and I asked them about the religion that they were greatly interested in and were trying to follow in their lives. Apparently, a lot of it centres around a man called Haile Selassie, the Emperor of Ethiopia, who to these people was something of a god, and I must admit that the more they told me the more interested I became in finding out more. They also told me about Marcus Garvy and, again, I have done a lot of reading in relation to this man's history, and it would seem that both men have been a wonderful inspiration for black people.

I became particularly close with three of the lads, Guy, Tony, and a young man nicknamed Roachy. I remember Roachy saying to me one day, "You're not such a bad bloke really, Philip. You should get yourself a book on The Lion of Judah, Haile Selassie. Maybe you'll find something of interest in it." I don't think Roachy realised it, but usually when anyone tells me anything like that I follow it up, so that night on my way back home I called in at the local library and borrowed a book on Emperor Haile Selassie. The very first page started off: Haile Selassie, born 23rd July! Everything in my life at that time over a period of about 18 months, whether it be at work or at home, seemed to be associated with 23rd July, my own date of birth. Perhaps it didn't have any real meaning and in fairness I have never found an answer to suggest any spiritual or psychic significance, but they were strange coincidences.

People talk of haunted houses and if ever there was a haunted house then Gipsy Lane was it! However, it was not in a bad way, to scare or unnerve you, because it was the friendliest little house with a warm, gentle atmosphere. Even my daughter, Nadine, whom it has to be said doesn't seem to be blessed with an inherent psychic ability, would tell us about the people she could see and talk to there. When she was about two years old she would frequently tell her mother of a little girl she talked to and played with called Wanda. I know that lots of children have similar experiences and invent friends, but I made very tentative enquires of Ivy, the next door neighbour, without suggesting my source, and she seemed to recall a family named Lycett who once lived there and had a daughter called Wendy but who was better known as Wanda.

My daughter also spoke of a dirty man, who had a black face and hands and whose clothes were covered in filth. My wife told me that one day she had gone upstairs to our bedroom to make the bed and Nadine had followed her up and gone into the playroom. Suddenly Nadine dashed into our room, slamming the door behind her and leaning on it as if someone were following her. When Kath asked her what was wrong, she said a dirty man had tried to pat her on the head. Kath took her by the hand and went back into the playroom, but she could see nothing. She looked quickly into our daughter's bedroom, which was also empty, and feeling rather perturbed she picked Nadine up and went downstairs to look in the other rooms. Again, there were no signs that anyone had been in the house.

As with all small children you have to wonder if it is their imagination or just something they have made up but, having come from a psychic background, this occurrence was always of great interest to me and I would never reject it out of hand. Then we had a very interesting connection about six months after the incident, when we demolished an old building at the rear of the house and dug it out to install new foundations. There we found an old miner's helmet and lamp. Could this have been the man with the black face and hands and dirty clothes? Again, Ivy confirmed that mining people had lived in the area.

On another occasion my wife was in the kitchen from where she could hear Nadine chatting away as though she were having a conversation with someone. Curious, Kath went to the doorway and asked her what she was doing. Our little girl was sitting in the armchair by the window and told her she was talking to an old man and said, "He's reading the paper," and she pointed to the armchair on the opposite side of the room. Suddenly, looking in the direction of the chair she asked, "Where are you going?" and then said, "Bye bye," and she started to wave and blow kisses. My wife asked her what was happening and Nadine explained matter-of-factly that the old man had told her it was time for him to go because he'd got to go to Jesus. It had all seemed perfectly acceptable to our little girl of three!

Across the road from our house was a railway line, a track that had been there for many years and, indeed, my own grandfather, Will, had been a platelayer for the railway and his brother, Dick, had been a foreman on that very line. My grandfather had a little hut there, which my mother called his fogging hut. He was always glad when it was foggy, as were the other men, because it meant they wouldn't have to work quite so desperately hard as usual and he could spend some time in his little hut.

It had been quite a busy line at one time with steam trains going backwards and forwards. When we lived there, however, we would only hear the occasional electric train pass by (quite a nerve-racking experience when we first moved in, because the whole street seemed to rock and the little houses we lived in shook as the trains went past). But on certain nights there would be a very strong smell of those old steam trains and it wasn't just something that as a psychic only I could smell; my wife also had the experience on many occasions and so did Ivy next door. Also, other people who lived in the street could recall hearing the old trains rumbling along the tracks and the distinctive smell that can only be associated with those old steam trains.

An experience we had that was more than a little unnerving happened one night when my wife woke me up to say that she thought we were being burgled and there was someone on the stairs. I sat up in bed and listened and there was undoubtedly something on the stairs. We were both very scared and, although I have never been frightened of anything supernatural or of a psychic nature, for sure I know there are people on this physical plane who can do you a lot of harm and I always kept a hammer under the bed just in case! I reached under the bed, picked up the hammer and started to climb out of bed, but Kath grabbed my arm and held me fast because whatever it was was coming up the stairs - one, two, three - each step getting closer and closer, until finally the door started to open. Quick as a flash, I jumped out of bed, switched on the light and raised the hammer, but to my amazement nothing was there. All we could hear was the sound of something running back down the stairs.

I raced quickly onto the landing and down the stairs with Kath very close behind me and rushed straight into the living room. There were no signs of a disturbance and not a door was open anywhere. We checked the front and back doors, which had bolts on them - they were still in place. We quickly looked in each room - nothing! We checked the windows, which were the old sash type. The cords were all broken through age and the windows were stuck fast, so they were impossible to open and there were no broken panes of glass.

Having checked everywhere thoroughly we were left with two possibilities of what might have come up the stairs and started to open our bedroom door: a ghost, or someone who had the ability to vanish into thin air. As I have never yet come across anyone with the latter ability, I would have to say that it must have been a ghost!

There was nothing untoward or unpleasant at that house though. All we really experienced were things from days gone by. Within our house I frequently saw what can only be described as spirits or ghosts, but they were always very pleasant.They didn't seem to be very aware of me in all honesty and seemed to be carrying on their daily business in much same way as me.

Eventually the time came when we sold our little house in Gipsy Lane and bought the bungalow we still live in today. There wasn't much money to spare in terms of the move and we borrowed the van of a friend who lived down the road for about a week to transfer what possessions we had to our new home and basically empty the house, and I spent the last couple of days on my own there.

On the night we were to hand the keys in to the Estate Agent, I took my wife, daughter and baby son into the house and we just had a last walk round to see what we thought. I felt quite depressed at leaving, Kath shed a few tears and Nadine was highly delighted to be going to a nice new bungalow but was sorry to leave behind the many friends she had in the lane.

We closed the door behind us but, rather than hand the key in that night like I should have, I hung on to it and went back the next day for a last look around our old home. As I went through the hall into the empty living room there was a tremendous sadness and I could feel tears and sense people upset at our moving out. I know it sounds hard to believe, but all the people that I had seen going through doors and living their lives in another time in the house all seemed to draw close together and stand around me in the room, not scaring or frightening me but very upset and sad to see us go. The ladies I had seen in and around the house from all sorts of different times, a very well-dressed lady obviously from a middle-class background, another lady from a different time who seemed very poor and didn't seem to have much of anything really, a tall gentleman in a high hat, and a mining couple all seemed to be standing around me. It seemed they were communicating to me that they wished we wouldn't leave and that we would change our minds and come back. But I replied to them on a telepathic level that it was time to move on and I thanked them for all their help and guidance and for allowing me to share what had, after all, been their home too. I know it is hard to believe and almost equally as hard to explain in words, but I'm sure that day the spirits gathered to wish me goodbye and to wish me well in my new life. They were very sad to see me go and I was equally sad to say goodbye to them, but I did and I, Kath and the children moved on to another phase in our life together. Whoever lives in that house in Gipsy Lane now, if they are reading this book, I hope it doesn't make them feel nervous or scared, because I can promise that whatever energy exists there it belongs to some lovely spirit people and they will only bring happiness and balance, and hopefully the same luck that I experienced while we were there.

When I was a boy I lived at 5 Shepwell Green, a building that no longer exists today, and that was a very spooky house and a place that really scared me when I was a little boy. We only lived there until I was about seven or eight, but some of the experiences I had there were very scary. Mom had lived there, as well as next door when she was a child, and I had access to both properties as her mother and father had lived in the one house which was then occupied by my aunt and uncle and my mom and her first husband had lived at number 5. Then a few years later she lived there with my dad and me as well.

Sometimes I would see things there that were very nice really. For instance, I often saw a little old lady sitting in a rocking chair. She was never aware of me, no matter how I tried to catch her attention or speak to her. As a little three-year-old I never had any success with her at all, although I did have much more success when I went in the front room! On more than one occasion I would see another little lady in the corner of the room who was sitting in a chair that seemed to me to be suspended about 12 feet off the floor, although in reality that was impossible because the ceilings were quite low; it was more likely four or five feet. She was very nice and friendly and I always remember that she wore a white shawl around her shoulders. She could see me because when I spoke to her she answered me.

I once said, "Hello there, who are you?"

I was quite surprised when she replied, "Can you see me, son?"

I responded, "Yes, of course I can see you. Who are you?"

She said, "Well, Philip, you could say that I am your great-grandmamma, I'm sure that would be adequate." And with that she waved to me and seemed to drift and fade away.

At times, like any other little boy of five or six, I could be very naughty and mom, although she was very loving, was also a very strict disciplinarian and if you were naughty you had to be punished. One of her favourite punishments if I'd been bad was to put me on the stairs that led from the living room to the bedrooms, close the door on me and leave me there. It was a very old-fashioned little two-up, two-down house, and the stairs were absolutely pitch black. Until this day I can't explain, because I wasn't really old enough to be aware of it, but this was a place where spirits would build up and, indeed, mom told me in later life that she had actually seen her first husband materialise in that same area. I must admit that it wasn't a place I liked to be - in fact it terrified me, for whenever I was there I would sense people whom I didn't like, watching me and standing close to me and I always thought it was very unfair of my mother, who was a brilliant medium and naturally aware of such things, to do this to me. For sure, though, it was a punishment that would usually stop me immediately from being naughty, for a time at least!

What I would do was to put my face into the corner where the two walls joined and just stay there frozen with fear until hopefully mom would let me come out. In later life I would tell my mother of the experiences I had on the stairs and say to her, "It was wrong of you to put me there because it was so scary." In fairness I think she regretted it as well, but I don't think she was aware that anything would really scare me or draw to me. Unfortunately they did, but I am sure that I was always protected and those that cared for me also drew close to me, especially Grandma Mary, who had passed to Spirit shortly before. She would say to me, "Turn into the corner and I will stand in front of you so you do not need to be scared, my lad." It was also at the top of those stairs that I saw the large Red Indian man with a bear's head covering his own and, although I am sure he was there to protect me and look after me, nevertheless he scared me as well.

I think there are places like that in certain houses where ghosts, spirits or whatever have the ability to build up. If you have an area like that you will probably find that it seems to be a very cold place. Eerie isn't it? Perhaps that's the right word, for a cold spot can bring about a sensation that sends a strong tingling feeling up the back of your neck and right down your spine. Those of you reading this book will probably know of somewhere in your own home or a place you have visited that is like that and I am sure you will understand what I am talking about.

Chapter 6
To the Father a Son

In the year 1984, everything looked well structured in my life. I was working in the daytime for NACRO (the National Association for the Care and Resettlement of Offenders) in Dudley. I had originally gone there to work as a supervisor and very quickly over five years had moved up to the position of training organiser after successive promotions. My wife, who is an intelligent lady, had returned to full-time education to study for her BEd in English Literature, hoping to teach primary school children and move away from the secretarial and administrative occupations she had followed previously in life.

One weekend we both decided we would have a bit of a break, me from writing up reports for work and Kath from the large amount of academic study, and we attended a local village fair. At the fair was a lady dressed as a fortune-teller who was charging a pound or two to tell people's fortunes.

Kath said, "Shall we go in?"

My immediate reaction was, "You must be joking! You know these people are charlatans. They all talk a load of rubbish. This has got nothing to do with psychic ability, mediumship or clairvoyance, they're just people out to make a crafty shilling, Kath."

"Oh, come on, let's go in, it'll be a laugh," she replied.

"All right then, if you insist," I answered.

She also insisted that I went first, so into the tent I boldly went and sat down opposite this rather strange gypsy-type lady.

"Give me your hand, my son," she said. I duly obliged, but as soon as she took my hand she immediately released it again. "Good God, have you got some psychic power!" she exclaimed.

Well, yes, I could accept that!

"Do you know that one day you are going to be very famous," she asked, "and have children that will make you very proud of them, one a great mind, the other a tennis player?"

Oh yes, thought I, I've heard all this before!

Suddenly she put her hands to her head and said, "I'm very sorry, young man, I can't work with you, you're just too powerful. Are you a medium?"

I said I thought she was probably right with that observation.

"I'll tell you one thing," she continued. "You will go on to be very famous and do this kind of work and I would like to wish you well."

"Yes, okay then," I answered as I handed my pound over to her and left the tent.

My wife then went in and I went off to have a look round the other stalls to see what else was on offer. Kath did spend a lot more time in there than I had, I must admit, and I thought she must be giving her a bit of the old flannel! However, when she came out she was rather flabbergasted by what she had been told. Apparently the gypsy woman had told her a lot about her past life that was very accurate, and she had also asked her if she was married to me. She could have guessed that, of course, as Kath had gone in right after me, but she told my wife that I was very psychic and very powerfully gifted. She also told my wife that she worked with children and could see many books around her, but that would change shortly and that she would work with one child and that some money she was going to receive would come from a different source than she expected. I think she had impressed Kath more by what she had said about her past, but she had also found the other prediction very interesting if not a little puzzling.

Two weeks later we went on holiday to Wales to a little town called Conway, which I had known very well in my younger years and so I enjoyed returning to it. My wife had also previously enjoyed it there very much, but not on this particular holiday. Kath felt unwell and sick a lot of the time and, whilst I took my daughter out and about quite a lot, Kath ended up not doing very much at all because she just didn't feel well enough. Then halfway through the holiday she suddenly announced to me that she thought she was pregnant.

"You can't be," I said, "can you?"

"Well, I shouldn't be," she answered.

My wife was on the Pill at that time and, although it is known to happen, falling pregnant is very unlikely. However, she seemed sure it was the case and decided to get one of the simple little pregnancy kits you can buy from the chemist. The results indicated that she was indeed pregnant. Not totally convinced, when we got home Kath went to see our family doctor and friend, Dr Paul Hammet Le Brun, who arranged for a pregnancy test that confirmed it. "Yes, indeed, my dear, you are definitely pregnant," he said.

Being halfway through her BEd degree studies, this was something of a shock to Kath to say the least. Of course there were possibilities that she could consider, for example a termination, but I knew my wife well enough to know that she would never take such action. If God had given us our child in that way then she would certainly have the baby, there was no doubt of that in her mind, but of course it meant the end of her teacher training and all her tutors and lecturers at college were very shocked and disappointed as she had shown a lot of promise. However, they were also very understanding and told her that she could go away, have the baby and would be given up to six years to go back and finish her degree. (As it happens, she never did return to college and is now back in secretarial work at the local University of Wolverhampton, which she enjoys very much.)

When the time came, we had a boy and called him Paul. I had always wanted a son really, but in truth my wife had no intention of having another child after our daughter Nadine was born. She felt she only wanted the one child and that we could offer better opportunities, help and support for just one child. However, Paul was very loved and welcomed into the family and he has been a blessing to us all really. My parents absolutely adored him, especially my mother, who was delighted with the new addition to the family and strangely, although Paul was only 2 years old when my mother passed to the higher life, he reminds me of her in many ways as he has many of her personality traits. He can be quite stubborn and yet very loving. He was a very sensitive child but delighted in practical jokes throughout his childhood, much I suppose as any young boy tends to do. Now we have reached the year 2007 and he has passed his twenty-first birthday, he is quite a serious person and I feel he has a natural healing gift that he may choose to show to others at some time in the future. For now, however, his life revolves around cars, his friends, music, and social life. Moody, but about as normal as you could get, I suppose!

Paul's unexpected arrival into this world has been the way of my life in recent years. We seem to be going along one way in a very straight, positive direction when something comes along to change it completely and, although financially things were a lot tighter back then, I must say that both his mother and I am so very, very glad that God decided to give him to us. It also makes me feel a bit guilty for prejudging the fortune-teller at that little village fair. I suppose over the years I have been lucky in as much as I have had readings off just about everyone, from some of those with a reputation as great mediums, psychics, astrologers, clairvoyants, palmists, tarot readers, etc., to ordinary housewives and men with a very natural gift and, on looking back, that little gypsy lady at the fair probably gave me about the most accurate reading that I have ever received, in all honesty. I was to become famous and I did go on to develop my psychic gifts, so I suppose she was right about my being a medium and having power whose vibrations she was unable to take on. She even told me that I had two children, even though neither my wife nor I knew that the second one was on the way. If she is reading this book, perhaps it is a good time for me to apologise and agree that she was right - to the father would come a son! And as for Kath, as she had predicted there certainly were lots of books around her at that time and there was something special about to happen involving children as, nearly 13 years after the birth of our daughter Nadine, our unplanned new arrival, our son Paul, was on the way.

Chapter 7
Philip Solomon the Ghost Hunter

For almost all of my life I have had a great interest in ghosts and hauntings and I think really that can easily be explained. My mother was a top local Spiritualist medium and greatly involved at the highest level with the local Spiritualist church at Darlaston in the West Midlands, and people were always coming along and telling her of their experiences and stories of what they called ghosts, and either by prayer, simple explanation or occasionally a visit to where they had had these experiences, mother would put an end to their problems or, alternatively, explain to them that they should not be nervous or scared of what they were experiencing.

However, I was very different from my mother in those days, and I am ashamed to say but openly admit that I wanted to prove that the majority of those people who came along with paranormal stories were pranks, cranks or at the very least just the sufferers of a vivid imagination, and readily took on the role of ghost hunter and researcher of the paranormal at mother's church. However, I very quickly realised that some cases just could not be explained away as simply as I thought; many could, but some could not be answered. Indeed, they could only be called ghosts, or at the very least unexplained phenomena.

As a top psychic consultant, let me put you clear on my position with regard to ghosts as I see the matter now, with an older and wiser perspective perhaps. I believe that ghosts are the memories of people who died, perhaps tragically, and are unaware of their own death or passing over. A ghost can be part of that person's personality left earth-bound in the atmosphere of their former existence and it usually appears at the same place over and over again. Strangely enough, ghosts seem to rarely travel any distance or leave the place in which they lived most of their lives. Spirits are different and can, and indeed do, travel around.

I hope I am not confusing you, and I also hope that you are not saying that ghosts and spirits are surely the same thing because they most certainly are not. Spirits are the surviving personalities of all of us that progress past death to the first stages of the higher life. I believe that we continue to proceed in an existence where we act out our lives, care, love and progress much as we had done in our earthly life except, of course, that it is on a higher dimension. Ghosts, however, can only repeat over and over again what were often the very final minutes of their life, or perhaps a pleasant or unpleasant experience, as repetitive obsession draws them to the earth plane and in many cases they are incapable of progressing to the higher first life.

In my experience as a ghost hunter I will say one thing: ghosts are nearly always completely harmless. However, do heed a warning: although there is nothing at all to be scared of, strange and unpleasant entities can be drawn to the vibration of an inexperienced researcher. I always used to advise those helping me who have had this experience to stop their research immediately and pass the work on to a professional medium or a psychic consultant or, of course, get in touch with their local Spiritualist church where in most cases there would be someone who knew what they were about and would be able to handle the situation. My research and work very much led me to believe that in the majority of cases ghosts, whatever they might be, draw energy from the living and they are especially likely to make themselves known to someone with psychic ability such as myself or if another similarly attuned psychic person is present. Indeed, the more psychics present the more likely an apparition would be to appear. This is also very relevant in terms of the phenomenon of moving objects such as a glass or the opening or closing of a door. When a manifestation becomes entirely physical in nature and can be observed by a lot of people it could be that a poltergeist haunting is under way. Time and time again my experience has led me to note that in these instances there are usually teenagers close by, approaching or passing through puberty, who have untapped energies that are unconsciously causing poltergeist-type activity. I believe that the sexual fluids are similar to the so-called ectoplasm produced by the physical mediums in controlled seances, especially in Victorian times. Some ghosts, even spirits, can be a little naughty just as they were in their earthly life and can cause problems.

Another completely wrong assumption is that ghosts only come out at night. My investigations clearly showed that they were just as likely to be seen during the day as in the dark of evening, although the less disturbance and the quieter the place the more appropriate the atmosphere would appear to be for a manifestation. My work also suggests that the anniversary of deaths and similar instances appear to make an indelible imprint on time and atmosphere, and spirits or ghosts that are locked in limbo tend to appear at these times. The only way to deal with these repetitive hauntings is if someone like myself or a trance medium makes contact with these people, yes people, and convinces them that they have passed over to another life and must move on, and this is basically all that is usually needed to change the understanding of these poor people. One word of warning: it is often done over a controlled time in a proper rescue circle and must not be attempted by amateurs and, indeed, never on your own.

People also ask me what sort of equipment I would use as a ghost hunter and I usually make them laugh when I tell them, but I have to be honest and tell you the truth too. We never had heat-sensitive cameras or professional video equipment, electromagnetic force meters, or electronic thermometers or anything of that nature back then. Usually one of us would have a large case containing a reporter's jotter, pencils, retractable ruler, a 12-inch wooden ruler, a digital watch that would light up at night, a good magnifying glass, a spool of black cotton, string, a small portable tape recorder, a roll of adhesive tape about 1 inch wide, a good thermometer (which again hopefully you could see clearly), a packet of chalk, talcum powder, a 1 inch paintbrush, a pencil sharpener and a camera with a built-in flash, preferably with an infrared lock, and no doubt you're now saying to yourself, what is all this stuff for?

So let me try to explain to you how I would use this equipment as a ghost hunter. The reporter's jotter and my pencils were what I would use to make notes and to record anything that happened. I would always honestly record the occurrences or sounds that were seen or heard. I would also note down whether it was witnessed by anyone else apart from myself, as well as the date and the precise hour and minute.

My magnifying glass was very important for examining footprints and handprints that could be invisible to the human eye. It was also very useful for the post-ghostly substances that might be left behind, and if you are laughing at my experiences and thinking that I must have looked something of a Sherlock Holmes-type character, well that is what I was, a ghost detective if you like. I would use the talcum powder in this way: if there was a cupboard, chair, table or some other object with a polished surface I would tip a small amount of the powder onto it and quickly blow the surplus away. Time and time again it would leave prints and, upon examination, of course most of them would be natural, but if something was supernatural then it would be clearly shown and there I would have a record. The key was to see if any of the prints were different from those that had been in the room or members of the family who lived there, or of course from my own team.

I would also carry chalks and they were very useful to me. For example, if I had reports of a chair that moved on its own, without telling anyone I would very carefully chalk around the legs. If someone claimed then that it had moved and I wasn't certain that it had, the chalk marks would definitely prove which one of us was right. The string, self-adhesive tape and lengths of cotton were for securing doors and sealing windows, although normally the self-adhesive tape would suffice. We would cut about four or five pieces of the tape into 2 to 3 inch lengths and place them over the gap between the door/window and the frame where claims had been made that they opened and closed by themselves. We would set a watch and see what happened. If we heard a bang or noise we would immediately put on the lights and any breakage of the tape would be self-evident. If there were no breakages we would look for some other cause for the noise. More often than not we were experiencing the 'prank or crank' syndrome!

I always carried a small tape recorder on every hunt so that it could be left running continuously in a particular room in the building we were investigating or staying in to see what it picked up and, with the permission of those involved I would also use it to record any interviews. It is surprising how easy it is for someone, even me, to find the unconscious or subconscious mind painting the situation far more lucidly than it really is. The tape recorder, however, does not have such problems and only tells the story as it is. The camera I always took with me was a simple model with a flash that would very quickly and automatically set itself to all conditions and operate at just a push of a button.

The thermometer was very important. I often found that when any psychic manifestation occurred, just before, during and just after the event the area around it would become very cold.

I must admit that my kit was very basic, but it comprised all I ever really needed to take with me. I felt you had to look at things individually. Perhaps I was lucky; I am naturally psychic and this gave me the advantage of seeing and being aware of what was before me and having an inner ability to suss out when people were trying to con me. I suppose at times I would appear to be a little strange or funny to some of my colleagues who had such equipment as video cameras, closed circuit TV, infrared telescopes, volt meters and highly technical paraphernalia to detect humidity and electromagnetic fields, and I am sure to offend some of those old friends by saying this but in my opinion some of the evidence that I found was just as good if not better than they achieved. For all the fancy equipment there is very little evidence that can be shown on film and on technically recorded equipment that proves the existence of ghosts or hauntings, and I believe the reason for this is that we have not yet developed the right type of equipment that is capable of recording these things, but I am sure that in the future we will. Indeed, just think what a shock it would be for our great-grandparents if they were in this world today and switched on a television to see the pictures and hear the words the way we do. They would not believe it possible.

The comment I always seem to receive from the media, general public and friends is how exciting it must have been to be a professional ghost hunter. Well, it wasn't really, you know. At times it could be tremendously boring. Hour after hour could be spent seeing or hearing nothing at all. You might hear a noise and jump up excitedly to activate your equipment only to find that it was the dog getting up for a stretch; or a chilling, whistling wind proved to be nothing more than an air brick behind a cupboard. Ninety-nine times out of a hundred I would find a natural answer rather than anything supernatural, but of course it is that unexplained one per cent that is very exciting and interesting to someone like me. It also has to be said that sometimes friends would ridicule and laugh at me, but when I started to research and look for ghosts seriously and admitted my interest to family, friends and workmates, I actually found many of them telling me about their experiences and ghosts they had heard of or seen.

In the early days I wrote to all the local newspapers, and the *Express & Star* in Wolverhampton and the *Evening Mail* in Birmingham were particularly helpful and both would often give me little write-ups in the paper that guaranteed lots and lots of letters would come in telling me of new stories. This, together with places that mom would pass on to me, would of course mean that I had many to look at, and although obviously many of them would quickly be dismissed as silly publicity-seeking efforts, some were worthy of further investigation. I also made myself known at this time to the local BBC radio station and quickly earned the title 'The Ghost Man', although that was something I never liked being called and still don't to this day. Would you?

I made many friends at all the local libraries, and the librarians in the local history departments were particularly helpful and would quickly guide me towards books, stories and legends and show me records or written reports relevant to hauntings old and new. I also regularly visited the county record offices, both local and further afield, and much of what I wanted to look at would be on microfilm. I also frequently read publications such as *Psychic News*, for which I am now a feature writer, and *Prediction Magazine* which always had stories worth looking at, and of course I always kept an eye on the local papers too for stories to investigate. The biggest newspaper in the West Midlands at that time, with the largest circulation in the UK, was the *Wolverhampton Express & Star*, for which I am also currently a feature writer. Interestingly, many ghosts seem to appear at important historical buildings that are usually open to the public. I would visit these and talk to the guides, who were usually only too pleased to tell me about any hauntings or ghosts, and if I was really lucky and showed my most professional attitude sometimes I even got invited to meet the owners who usually had one or two little secrets that had been kept hidden and not investigated. Where a building was owned by the National Trust there would usually be little booklets or pamphlets, which were very helpful to me in my detective work.

You are probably wondering by now: how would you basically go about an investigation? So let me give you an illustrative example. Let's say I have been told about the so-called ghost of a soldier that appears regularly at the rear of the local pub. The story has been passed on by the friend of a friend who claims to have seen this ghost on numerous occasions. Step one sees me visit my friend and his/her friend and listen very carefully to the tale they have to tell. I listen to that story without any prompting or interruption or at least with the very minimum of open-ended questions. I make sure that I take notes and tape record the interview and also ask them if they have had any other ghostly experiences and if they know of anyone else who has actually seen the ghost. On my notepad I write down my observations as to whether the person being interviewed seems stable or of an excitable or imaginative nature. I try to be honest and use my basic intuition rather than tune in psychically. When I get home I replay the interview and write out a detailed report which is then filed in an index for future reference.

My next move is to visit the place where the haunting is alleged to be taking place. I try to make sure I am accompanied by a friend or someone that I can trust (I would usually take my old friend Marsha Barnes on this type of visit) and of course take my case containing the ghost hunter's tool kit. We then see if we can hear or see anything for ourselves and record our own feelings: did we feel excited, was there a clammy feeling, were we cold or unusually hot? All this information from our investigations then goes into a final report irrespective of whether we have heard or seen anything or not.

On occasions it would not be possible to visit in person or get a colleague or friend to do likewise, and in that instance I would write to all concerned, always enclosing a stamped addressed envelope, asking for all details of what was happening, but it was never as successful a way of looking at ghosts and hauntings as a one-to-one interview and never proved entirely satisfactory. I always found that a short investigation into the history of any site we were looking at, whether it was a building or a piece of land, was very helpful and the local records office would be a starting point for this sort of investigation, they hold land records and tithes from a very early date, and even a specific details of people who lived in buildings on particular pieces of land dating as far back as 1841 on the census returns, which have been taken every ten years right up until the present time. Unfortunately it must be said that these records for last hundred years remain legally non-viewable, although a well-presented reason to the authorities usually got me access to this information and details such as the comparable then/now layout of buildings, roads, footpaths, streams, mines and even wells.

Well and mine locations seem to produce lots of stories about ghosts and on numerous occasions I have been extremely disappointed to find that a regular moaning noise, and even the opening and closing of doors, was nothing more than the result of subsidence that had clearly been proven to be caused by underground mining in the past. Ninety-nine per cent of cases have similar easily explainable answers to suspected hauntings.

Sometimes, however, matters were different and the reason for a ghost or haunting could be found by looking into the history of a building or family. This was often the case in my investigations where buildings had been occupied by several generations of the same family, and on many occasions I have offended someone by uncovering an old family 'skeleton in the cupboard' that is directly related to a present-day haunting. I have even found myself threatened with everything from solicitors to shotguns, strangely enough often by the very people who had brought me in to investigate it in the first place!

However, I always had four rules that generally kept me on the right side of most people and, indeed, on the right side of the law. Firstly, I was always totally honest and straightforward when approaching anyone for the first time and following up a lead for investigating a case. Secondly, I always obtained permission in writing from the relevant individuals, including an SAE, before visiting any private building or land. If I received no reply I would leave the case alone. Thirdly, I think it is fair to say that I have never been tempted to exaggerate or distort the truth, and those that do end up discredited and, worse still, tend to tar the reputation of all the genuine researchers, among whom I include myself, with the same brush. Finally, I was always courteous, well-mannered and I hope, above all, professional, and that I believe probably more than anything else is how I managed to get the stories that I have related in several of my books, such as *Ghosts of the Midlands and How to Detect Them* and *Ghosts, Legends and Psychic Snippets*, and will be included in my latest project, an encyclopaedia of the ghosts of the British Isles, in which I shall try, or perhaps contrive would be a better word, to show you the way to see or detect ghosts for yourself, because if you have the sort of inside information and basic tool kit that I have described in this chapter, it is not as hard to do as some parapsychologists or ghost hunters would have you think.

Chapter 8
Friends

In 1987, I met by chance (I'm joking, of course, as nothing ever happens by chance, especially in my life!) a couple who were to become very special friends - Marsha and Dennis Barnes. One evening I had gone along to Wolverhampton Spiritualist Church where my father, Howard, was taking a service and giving a demonstration of clairvoyance. Marsha and I, in particular, became firm friends and I believe we will remain so forever. We both agree that we knew each other in previous lives. She is a very psychic lady and, amazingly, even in those very early days of our friendship she told me her opinions of my past lives, which I consider accurate and they fit in well with what I have been told by other mediums, psychics, clairvoyants, etc. She also often accompanied me on home visits to members of the general public for private consultations. I always found Marsha to be a very balancing lady and at times it is helpful to have someone like that come along with you.

Marsha is, without a shadow of a doubt, my greatest supporter and she has helped me in other ways too. As an example, I once had a very upsetting experience when, around 1988, a young Shropshire girl went missing. The media and newspapers made it clear they felt the worst had happened to her and she might be dead. One night, I had a dream of seeing my grandfather as a boy running away from the railway station at Highley village in Shropshire, close to the farm where he had lived as a child until the turn of the twentieth century. In the dream he was upset and was trying to warn someone that something was wrong in the river. I knew somehow that it had something to do with the missing girl. The next day I told Marsha of my dream and that I felt they would find the girl in the river at Highley. The following day the newspapers and television news duly reported that this was exactly what had happened: the girl's body had been found in the River Severn at Highley. Of all the villages in Great Britain, and there must be thousands, I had hit it spot on.

At the time I just kept wondering why, if my grandfather was able to let me know that her body was there, he had not let me know something sooner so that I could have helped her in some way, or maybe even saved her. This affected me so badly that for a while I decided I would give up my work as a psychic medium altogether - Philip Solomon Psychic Consultant would be no more. I felt my gifts had no meaning. What use was it to receive information like that when it was too late to do anything for the poor girl? Marsha was very supportive at that time and talked me round to looking at it from a different angle. There was nothing that I could have done. The young lady was already dead; she had been in the river for some time. If no one had found her then perhaps I would have been able to speak out so that at least her parents would have known what had happened to her. Gradually I came to accept these words of wisdom and decided it was my duty to carry on with my psychic work.

Another great friend and a very special man whom I worked with in the early eighties was Jim, a former professional soldier. We operated together for about five years, helping and working alongside ex-offenders, usually really tough, rough and ready young lads, who could be difficult to work with. We would take them on projects such as building work, gardening, painting and decorating, etc. Sometimes we would go to old people's homes, help the disabled or get them involved in community work that other people didn't want to do, these kids included! The organisation we worked for was called NACRO (The National Association for the Care and Resettlement of Offenders) and at that time it was about the only organisation around with the aim of helping those who had been in trouble with the law. It was understandable in some ways because it has to be said that some of the lads could be a real handful at times and very difficult to deal with. Many had a history of violence and most had been put away in care or had police records behind them. However, if I say so myself, we worked miracles with them, basically because Jim and I had the same outlook on life. The way to reach these lads was through showing them respect and that we cared about them.

I will give you an example, but have changed the lad's name so as not to embarrass him. Jim, myself and about six lads were sitting around a campfire waiting for a kettle of water to boil. One lad, 'Sam', was being an absolute pain in the backside, bullying the other lads and being more than a little threatening to Jim and me.

I looked over to him and asked, "Why don't you care about people and stop acting the way you do?"

He glared in my face and shouted, "Nobody cares about me, do they?"

"I do, Sam," I replied, "and as long as I have this job, and I know that goes for Jim as well, whatever you do we will always try to help you."

Sam looked at me, then at Jim, and then round at the boys. He obviously had a tear on one cheek and was clearly about to cry. But he didn't. He stood up, kicked the kettle off its stand and stormed away. But that lad never gave me another minute's trouble and particularly related to me throughout the rest of his training and, indeed, he has gone on to do well for himself in life, being very successful in the field of professional boxing and business.

His case was not unusual, as Jim and I saw many instances of lads who reacted in much the same way but eventually managed to go on and make something out of life for themselves, and I think the results our partnership achieved probably amazed Jim even more than they did me. He would often say to me, "Phil, surely we must have been chosen to do this. Do you think we are placed here to do it? Is it something to do with that Karma thing you talk about?"

Jim often talked about The Beatles. He seemed to think they had been placed on earth with a special gift and that there was more to them than just their music. Indeed, he felt they were beings placed here to help bring about love and peace in the world. They were, Jim, but so were you, and you did that work very well. Today, Jim works at the Central Television Studios in Birmingham, teaching young stars the skills of radio and television and hoping, I would think, that they will use the media to be soldiers in the army of love and peace as he knew The Beatles should have been and, I think, probably would have been had John Lennon survived.

My friend, David Icke, is a man who has had his fair share of publicity, some very good, some very bad. But I found that the old saying, 'You can only speak as you find', applied to David, and I have always got along very well with him and I am pleased to call him a friend. Of course, I had

Mary Ann, Philip's maternal grandmother, a fine medium, at Blackpool

Moody Dude! Philip in 1971

Philip, at five years old, pictured right

Elsie Saunders, President of Darlaston Spirtualist Church, pictured centre

1951, Philip Solomon arrives, pictured in the arms of his granma, Mary

Philip's mom, Elsie, a truly great medium in the ATS during the war years

Top Right: Philip looking absolutely fabulous in the late sixties!

Right: When not demonstrating mediumship, he's signing Rock 'n' Roll

Philip's graduation with his family gathered round

Elvis and Viva Las Vegas.
It's Phil in the States!

Off to Buckingham Palace to take tea with the Queen.
A very proud day for Philip, 2004

Derek Acorah and Philip, working together at Granada

Philip Solomon takes a look into his crystal ball

Philip Solomon demonstrating
mediumship in the theatre

Philip and Russell Brand investigate the Rosslyn Chapel

seen him many times around the various radio and television studios in the Midlands and Birmingham areas and he always seemed a friendly and jovial sort of chap, yet serious and considered by many in the broadcasting industry a certainty to reach the very top, but I only got to know David really well after I read a book he had written called *The Truth Vibrations*. Prior to that I probably had preconceived ideas about the man and probably based my views on what others had said about him. After reading this book, however, it seemed to me that he shared a lot of my own views. He certainly seemed to say a lot of the words that my mother had spoken and outlined many years before. I wrote to congratulate him on the book and he immediately wrote back asking if I would telephone him. When I did, he invited me to the next meeting of the Green Party in Wolverhampton, at which he was to speak, and after delivering a very well-received speech David and I spent quite some time together discussing our different points of view on the spiritual and psychic world and the like. However, on arriving home that night I had something of a shock: on the front page of the Wolverhampton evening newspaper, the *Express & Star*, was a picture of David and me beaming out for all to see, and really we have remained friends ever since.

David is certainly a man who speaks whenever the time inspires or moment takes him. He once phoned me at 7 o'clock in the morning just to talk about a chain of thought he'd had. He was also very complimentary about me in his autobiography, recalling the time I met him at the Hippodrome Theatre. We had agreed to meet for lunch and a chat with his agent, Paul Vaughan, also a good friend and a man who was interested in promoting talks by David around Great Britain following the media attention he had received and the publication of his autobiography. I asked David if he knew he would be playing football again shortly.

"Me?" he said. "Don't be crazy. With this arthritis and these hands I'll never play football again, Philip!"

"You will," I answered. "You definitely will!"

I asked him to let me look at his hands and I then placed mine over them and repeated, "You will play again, David, I promise you."

About a week later my telephone rang quite late one night. It was David Icke. "You're bloody amazing!" he exclaimed. "Guess what? You know I'm president of the Isle of Wight football club, well, the goalkeeper's injured and I'm playing in the next match!"

"I told you so, David," I answered. "I knew that you would, and I promise you that your hands will be much better now than they have been for a long time. I don't publicise my healing gifts but, take it from me, they will be much better."

That year, in my annual New Year predictions for the *Sunday Mercury*, the Midlands' own Sunday newspaper, I said that David Icke would be taken a lot more seriously in the future, and I believe that has happened. He has written numerous books and made several television documentaries, and now we have reached 2007 people do seem to be listening more to what he has to say.

Another night David telephoned me at home, again quite late. "How are you, mate?" he asked in his inimitable way.

"Not so bad really," I said, "but I'm a bit moody to be quite honest. I've got a feeling there's bad news coming about India. A lot of bloodshed and bad vibrations in that part of the world."

Then we just talked about general things, such as our wives, children, etc. The very next day, however, the world's press was filled with the news of India where there were riots, bloodshed, and there had even been an attack on the Sikh Golden Temple, just as I had thought when I had spoken to David the night before on the phone.

David has always been very fair to me and relates most of these predictions in one or other of his books. I have always found him to be a man who speaks out honestly about what he believes to be the truth. Perhaps those he really offends are the staid and orthodox, and those who are unchallengeable and unchangeable in their fixed views, but nothing ever changes without someone challenging it first and David has always been prepared to do that! I, for one, respect him for it.

I've always been a bit like that really and looked for the friendship of those that others have castigated, maybe because they haven't understood them. I well remember when the Duchess of York was having such a terrible time with the media and almost everyone seemed to be challenging her, picking on her and blaming her for everything that went wrong in the royal family. My view was that she is basically a very good lady and I made the prediction that one day she will be one of the most popular women in the land. I still stand by that prediction and at the height of her problems I was prompted to write to her to tell her what I thought. I received a very nice letter in reply, personally signed 'Sarah', thanking me for my heartfelt words which had brought her comfort in a time of great difficulty.

I have received hundreds of similar letters both from celebrities, show-business people, the aristocracy and also everyday, ordinary people, and they are all equally important and meaningful to me and they are always a pleasure to receive, knowing that I have helped.

It is strange really, but people always seem to come into my life who will help me too, especially along the spiritual and psychic pathways, guiding my career and pushing me on. One gentleman who perfectly fits that bill is the great Austrian scientist and writer of many books (115 I think, at the last count), Dr Professor Hans Holzer. I first started to write to Hans Holzer after reading a very interesting feature that he wrote for a magazine in America called *Fate*, which is very similar in many ways to our own *Prediction Magazine* in England, of which I am a big fan.

Surprisingly, I received a letter back from Professor Holzer asking if I would do a written reading for him and if I would do a few of my psychic snippets on what I thought would be there for him in his immediate life as well. I agreed to his wishes and, without going into the private details of what I had told him, he wrote back saying that he was very surprised by the accuracy of what I had said. Indeed, he described me as an amazing man and asked me to write back with some more, which I did. Again, he wrote back to tell me what I had written was spot on and once again asked for more!

I think it is fair to say that Professor Hans Holzer has always been impressed with my work, so much so that he asked me if I would consider getting in touch with his English agent and personal friend, Mr Jeffrey Simmons, a man who lives close to Belgrave Square in London. Professor Holzer was quite adamant and insisted that my work was of such a high standard that it must be brought to the attention of Mr Simmons, and an appointment duly led to a meeting in London. Jeffrey suggested that we should consider a five-year plan that focused on my writing a collection of books to be brought to the attention of the British public and, hopefully, the world.

Finally, Jeffrey said to me, "You know, Philip, I have worked with some of the greats. I helped Uri Geller to publish his first book, I handled Russell Grant and Patrick Walker for a time, and also helped Doris Collins write her books. I'm Michael Bentine's agent now and when I was a publisher I published books by such people as Matthew Manning and Ena Twigg. You've got a dynamic personality and, this is a funny thing to say, but I can see a lot of George Formby in you!"

Now that struck me because I'm not really keen on being likened to George Formby - wasn't he a comedian and singer?! But if I could get the stardom and fame he had, I wouldn't mind that! It would give me the chance to speak to the world with, hopefully, words of wisdom. I also believe that comedians or those who can make you smile and laugh are the greatest of healers. Jeffrey looked at me again and said, "You know, you could be as successful as Doris Collins."

Quick as a flash I looked back at Jeffrey and said something I shouldn't have really, and I have regretted it ever since in many ways: "Jeffrey, I'm ten times better than Doris Collins now." As I said it I meant it and I thoroughly believed it, although I have to add that Doris Collins was a very wonderful medium and a marvellous healer too. It was not about our being in competition; everyone with an interest in the psychic and spirit world should come together and work together to improve and help mankind, and perhaps the silly comment I made proved I had some new lessons to learn quickly at that time, because for about two weeks afterwards I was absolutely hopeless and couldn't achieve anything at all, mediumistically at least. Just as quickly, though, I got it all back and I was as good as ever.

Perhaps the spirit world had decided to teach me a very quick, sharp lesson after my visit to the top literary agent, Jeffrey Simmons. They might have done, you know, because they are wise old friends as well as teachers and sometimes we all need to learn a lesson no matter how well we feel we have progressed as mediums and psychics!

Things were to go in another direction too. I was not to sign to Jeffrey Simmons' Literary Agency. Professor Hans Holzer was to take much more of an interest in my career as a writer and suggested that he should show my work to Bob Friedmann, who was the owner of Hampton Roads publishing company in Charlottesville, USA. Hans had come up with the idea that we should co-write a book, explaining what the spirit world is really like. This was the first time that a highly respected parapsychologist and a leading Spiritualist medium had compiled a book together of this kind, and it was subsequently published under the title of *Beyond Death: Conditions in the Afterlife*. It was a tremendous success in America and led to me spending quite a bit of time over there and being interviewed by some major names in the media, including New York legendary broadcaster, Joe Franklin, a fantastic man who also became a good friend, and many US shows such as Whitley Strieber's programmes about the paranormal. I had started off by looking for a publishing deal in London and yet found myself writing for American people, and I particularly enjoyed working in New York where I now have many dear friends.

I believe that some of our greatest friends are the pets we decide should come and join us in our homes and in many ways I think that they choose us. I also believe that animals, and particularly pets, are very psychic too. Many people ask me if I have any stories of psychic experiences involving animals and pets and I always answer that I do and, yes, often my own pets too. But I believe almost everyone could cite examples of these lovely creatures being gifted in such ways if we stop and think about it. I certainly believe the pets who are close to us are clairvoyant, clairaudient and clairsentient and communicate with us telepathically on many levels.

Throughout history there are reports of animals that have predicted danger. Even wild animals are said to leave earthquake areas and rats will escape flooded or burning buildings far sooner than the turmoil actually arrives in their location, and people who look after animals, such as zookeepers, have reported animals being disturbed and reacting well before electric storms or thunder occur.

In my various newspaper columns I have told stories about our old fox terrier dog, Lady, who always waited at the door for me to return home at unusual hours of the day or night, and this seems to apply to other people and their pets too. As you can imagine, the nature of my career means that I can be returning home from my work at the strangest of hours and I can even be away for days on end, but somehow Lady always seemed to know when I was close to home and insisted on going to the front door to wait for me, and she would become very agitated if she wasn't allowed to!

I told you earlier that when I was a small boy I owned a German shepherd dog called Bronco and he could certainly see Spirit and would sometimes draw my attention to them before I was aware of them myself. I remember once being in the park and being approached by a man who offered me sweets and wanted me to go with him. Despite being in my charge, Bronco growled at him and made it absolutely clear to me that I wasn't going anywhere with this person! Who can say, maybe he saved my life that day?

Mom and dad also bred poodles as a sort of part-time occupation and another lovely character was to come my way almost by accident. One of the bitches had a litter of puppies and one of them was not what you could call the prettiest of poodles; in fact she was a very strong, broad-headed, bullish-looking character when she grew up! But I loved her as a puppy and as no one would buy her she became mine. Her name was Tina and this particular dog absolutely adored me all her life. The only problem was that she was very possessive over me and friends who came to my house had to be very careful not to seem to be offending me in any way or even gaming around with me, for certainly such actions would leave them in danger of being badly barked and growled at and, sad to admit it, possibly bitten. There was only one exception and that was my girlfriend and future wife, Kath, whom for some reason Tina immediately liked - perhaps she knew Kath would become a part of my life.

Later on, when my daughter Nadine was born, Tina took on the role of nursemaid, lying under her carrycot and permanently guarding my little girl, and woe betide anyone who went anywhere near her. When we left to start up our own home, Tina was very old and suffering from cancer. Unfortunately, as we had a newborn baby and other commitments, she couldn't come with us and in many ways Tina never really got over this, but visits home were always special to her. A reassuring message for me after she passed was when Kath had a dream of seeing Tina with her late grandmother in spirit. This lady, I am told, was a very nice person who always had a dog herself and this helped me greatly to get over Tina's loss, especially knowing she was with someone who would love her on the other side.

A very unusual experience I had when I was a little boy involved a cocker spaniel bitch, which had been bought by my parents for breeding purposes but sadly died from distemper. I loved this little dog and had taught her many tricks such as how to fetch a ball, sit, beg, etc., and I couldn't get over her loss. One day in my bedroom I saw that little dog crystal clear, running from one side of the room to the other, and from that day on I was all right about her passing.

When young I also kept pigeons, tumblers and tipplers which fascinated me. I also had a large red and blue macaw that frequently used to call to me and say, "Pick it up, Philip." No doubt it had frequently heard this command being given to me by my mom and dad when I left things lying about as most lads do.

Kath and I also had an African grey parrot called Charlie, which had originally been bought for my daughter but he had decided that the only person he would have any time for was Kath. He would frequently open his own cage and quite happily come out and sit on her head or shoulder, but would screech at and peck everyone else in the household!

I hold the belief that pets often communicate with us on various levels and I am sure that all the ones I have told you about in this chapter did with me. Our last pet was a little Jack Russell terrier, Katy, who was with us for many years into her old age. After we had her put to sleep because she was suffering badly from cancer and blindness, I had a feeling that troubled me. I sensed her around the house and with us all the time and she couldn't understand why she wasn't getting patted or spoken to. One day I am quite sure that our old dog, Lady, came and took Katy to the other side and, yes, I do believe that all pets go to the spirit world and they are with us again when we go to the other side. Katy was never sensed very much after that; well, apart from the occasional scratching at the back door or rustling of little feet, and those occasional little visits are most welcome.

An interesting story I heard concerns a BBC broadcaster and the late medium, Doris Stokes, who had been staying at his home prior to a show. The gentleman in question had two Siamese cats which, whilst sitting alongside Doris, both looked in unison first to the left, then to the right, at something that had certainly captivated their attention but was not viewable by the broadcaster. Doris immediately told him not to worry about this as they could see spirit as could most animals, and this is a story that this particular presenter continues to tell to this day.

Lots of experiments have been conducted to test whether or not animals do possess paranormal powers, usually using Zener cards, which are the standard extrasensory perception (ESP) testing tool. Some very talented dogs have reportedly achieved over 70 per cent accuracy when asked by their owners to tap a particular and relevant card.

It should also be remembered that many creatures possess much more highly attuned senses than human beings. It is a fact that a homing pigeon taken from its home for the first time, for example living in England and released in France, will immediately fly back to its home and loft. Bats use highly developed distance-locating abilities to fly in the pitch dark without hitting a wall or tree. Ponies and horses are also often blessed with the ability to find their way home by purely using inner instincts and senses that we do not really understand, and dogs lost in one part of the country have been known to travel hundreds of miles to find their owners when they have moved to new homes. Surely this must be definite proof of their using psychic abilities.

I am sure many of you must have had similar experiences with your pets and other animals and think of them as I do, in many ways, as friends too.

Chapter 9

Enter the Guides

I wrote this particular chapter in response to a request from Hans Holzer's friend, the literary agent, Jeffrey Simmons. "People want to know what the guides are in Spiritualism, and what the term means," he said to me one day in London.

"That's a very difficult thing to explain, Jeffrey," I replied. "For, in all honesty, spiritual guides are so developed it is almost impossible to describe them accurately. For many they are what could be called friends from the spirit world, those who guide and help us in our life, and to some extent that is what they are."

But Jeffrey was really asking me about MacDonald and Marian. They are communicators from a much higher dimension than the realms I think he was referring to, but I will do my best. In fairness, I have questioned these two guides, but I think they are more interested in what they can do for me and how they can help me and show me how to progress and assist others in my lifetime rather than wasting time explaining themselves.

However, there is some information I can give you and this is it. MacDonald had at one time on this earth plane been a warrior chieftain who had four daughters but no sons, his first name being Carrig and his wife's Tanet. He told me that he passed to spirit, in that life, as a result of injuries received in a battle, not on the field but several days later. He described the location and church where he had been buried as a place where you could look out on a clear day and see the island of Iona off the Scottish coast. During my experiences of development as a very young man, MacDonald would sometimes tell me that it was his job to lead a team of other guides that would help and assist me on my pathway and in the work I had to do in my life, often influencing me. "Ye and I are one and the same, laddie. Trust me and I shall never put thee wrong." He told me that if I ever needed advice or communication with the spirit world or assistance psychically it was to him I should send out my thoughts and he would always draw close.

I have always been a great reader and one who would search out knowledge about the spiritual and psychic world generally, but MacDonald would always indicate that this was a mistake and I should be guided by my own inner understanding and influences that I would receive from him and others. This was particularly true for me, I believe, when I found myself having some difficulties fitting into the traditional Spiritualist movement and MacDonald assured me this was a perfect example of what the influence he was bringing to me meant. Basically, a lot of the information given out by so-called psychics or those that believe themselves to be sensitive to the spirit world can be misleading and contradictory, and only the guides, those that all of us have and who are specific to each individual, really have the wisdom to help that person, and for me MacDonald has always answered my questions, helped me to make the predictions that would allow me to be well enough known to reach others and been willing to pass on the knowledge he knew I would need to guide me at particular times in my life. In truth, even as I write this book, I would say that the influence of MacDonald is really strongly with me, perhaps not entirely channelling the work but guiding me to commit the words to print.

If I sound sceptical about the large number of books that have come out that are claimed to be channelled work passed on directly from a spirit force, then so be it, but I do not believe that is entirely a truth. I think we are influenced and guided rather than ever taken over completely by those on the other side, and in the end we make our own decisions about anything that we do in this life. I have always remained sceptical and questioning of what I know to be the truth myself. A good example is when I was going through a very difficult period in my life and as always in those times I sensed MacDonald close to me.

"Philip, laddie," I felt him say to me. "It is clear to us this is a difficult time in your life and you are very sceptical towards me, Marian and all those who would help you and I understand the way you feel. Remember that I have had many lives and have spent time on the earth and I know how difficult it can be to get by at times. I would encourage you to keep that open, questioning mind; that mind that makes you the researcher to sort out the chaff from the wheat. This is what has drawn other spirit helpers towards you, as they know that it will help them in helping you to show that there are many fraudulent people, con artists and charlatans, but you know that your clairaudience and your contact with me is good and true and that I will never let you down. The staff that I carry in my hand is a stout, strong stick and those that hurt, offend and criticise you will feel my wrath and the wrath of those that love me and thee."

Often I have asked the question of MacDonald, "How should I describe you, my friend?"

"Do you need to describe me?" is always the answer that comes back.

How would you describe any other true friend, except as someone you can always go to, talk with and trust, knowing that the advice they give you will only be to help you and never to harm you. That is how you would describe a true friend and that is what your main guide is really, the truest altruistic friend you will ever be aware of, if you are lucky enough to know of that awareness.

In earlier parts of my life I have asked MacDonald, "Can you not prove your existence by letting me see you?" For never in all my life have I ever seen MacDonald and yet, strangely enough, my wife has. Perhaps, as he says, we are so very close that we are part of one whole and the same tree or stick, and thus it is quite impossible for me to see him. My mother in her life also saw MacDonald and told me about the way he looked. The description given by my wife was exactly the same!

I once asked MacDonald if I could see the place where he lived on this earth. He replied, "Yes. In 1995 you will go to visit the Scottish Highlands and feel a sense of déjà vu, for the remains of my spirit still abound in and around the hills and mountains of the Scottish Highlands. Do not look for my place of burial, for that has no significance or meaning whatsoever. Like the shell you describe as a body, Philip, once the spirit or spark has left it, it is completely worthless and of no use whatsoever."

That was one of the few times I ever questioned the words of MacDonald, because I didn't expect to go to Scotland that year and I communicated this to him (finances and business commitments made it very unlikely).

"Philip, have I ever told you wrong?" came through the influence. "Have I ever been wrong in anything I have ever given you?"

I had to admit that he hadn't, and within a week my wife had told me she had found a bargain holiday to the Scottish Highlands and that we would be going for a short break in August. Once again MacDonald proved to be correct and, as always, I was wrong as far as he was concerned. It was a very pleasant place and we travelled all round the islands, and for me it was indeed very much a case of déjà vu, a feeling of being there before. I took MacDonald's advice and didn't try to tune in to or try to find the place he had been buried and I came away from Scotland feeling recharged and ready to get on with my work, perhaps even more focused as a professional medium.

I also frequently asked MacDonald about myself, such as what were my past lives and whether he and I are one, and he has always answered me, "When you die, Philip, as the great masters have taught you and others, there is no death. Read the words of Krishna, Buddha or Jesus Christ and all the prophets. Their words prove this and their lives would have had no meaning if it were not so."

Apparently, every time you live a life on earth you reincarnate and your spirit force or soul enters a new vessel or body. When you die that body becomes useless, and, like a worn-out jacket, it is discarded and you put on another one. MacDonald told me that, like everyone else, I have had a very long past and, by learning, suffering and facing problems, I have grown spiritually to a better level of understanding. He would always say to me, "You are lucky, Philip, that you are a very highly developed and attuned soul and your progression is now accelerating to a very high level of understanding. Perhaps you may not have many more lives to go, perhaps this is the last life you will have before you join us as an ascended master on the higher level, but I am not prepared to give you that information."

It was a very interesting snippet I received that day, though, for I always remember well before she passed to the higher life my mother had told me, "Son, once I pass over know that you will have no contact or any messages from me. The guides have told me I have done my work on this earth plane and now I am moving on. Do not miss me, I know the physical loss will be very hard for you to accept, but you do need to understand that I am progressing and moving on and have no wish, unless I absolutely have to, to come back and live on this earth plane again." Mom had had a hard time of it for sure and her words and the influential words that MacDonald was now giving to me fitted into a perfect pattern of understanding.

Understanding this pattern, which I suppose Eastern religions would describe as reincarnation, also means understanding what any psychic would call Karma, which basically is the philosophy that what we do in this life and other previous lives determines what will happen to us or how we will progress in future ones. Karma is the spiritual law of cause and effect. Eventually, if there is no cause, then it will not show the effect it has on individuals or their surroundings, and perfection is achieved, if you like. MacDonald always makes it very clear to me that I am the decision maker or master of my own destiny and, like all others, I must understand the consequences of my own actions.

"So who are you, MacDonald?" I would often ask.

"That's not for you to know, laddie. I have lived many lives in many places and I have told you of my association with Scotland and the life I lived there. The rest of my experiences in your world were my spiritual progression. Nay, lad, concentrate on your own life and, when you join us, then will be the time we shall talk of matters old and matters new!"

"So who was I then, MacDonald?" was another question I often asked in my earlier years.

Many people who believe in reincarnation or past lives often seem to imagine they were very famous: Cleopatra, Boadicea, Viking kings and queens, Sitting Bull or the chief of some other famous Indian tribe all seem to be favourites. So I was amazed when MacDonald told me that in one life I had been a famous king, a very wise king at that, and that I had also been a famous astrologer. This shocked me really, because I never make such claims or give their names and I will not do that now because they are private to me and are part of my own progression.

MacDonald also told me that I had lived as a farmer, not very far from where I live now, and that I had had a very hard life as I had been made an orphan at a very early age and had had to work very hard to become a successful tenant farmer. I had also been a boxer, an unsuccessful bare-knuckle fighter who had taken far more beatings than I had ever won fights! Also I had lived the life of a doctor, yet had wasted my talents, keeping the company of loose women and drinking myself to an early death. I have also been a miner, a stonemason and a lowly beggar who had to scavenge, steal, beg and borrow to survive. Perhaps that makes sense really, for if I had been a king then I would also have had to be a beggar to understand both sides of the coin. No king could really understand or have sympathy with someone who begged and lived on the street unless they experienced it for themselves. No lowly person could fail to be jealous of the life of a king until they knew how restricted a king's life might be and the decisions he would have to take and the life he would be forced to live: not being able to marry for love but rather to better your country; never being able to walk alone or talk to or meet the subjects that you hoped would love you without a permanent escort to protect you in the beautiful countryside over which you were the king. I think if I had been a king in a past life then I would also have had to be a beggar to reach proper progression.

"Have I had the experience of living the life of a woman, MacDonald?"

"You have not, laddie," he answered. "But Marian, your other trusted guide, has always been close to you and brought into your life the feminine side of you. Marian is a very old soul who has drawn close to you in almost all of your lives and she is the one who has made you sensitive, caring, gentle and understanding when that terrible temper of yours has come to the fore, but perhaps I have played a part in that temper on occasions!" And MacDonald heaved a great laugh as he said these words.

I don't communicate with Marian in the same way as I do with MacDonald. With her it is more an experience of sensing a caring, gentle, almost motherly influence, and she has been there with me since I was a little boy. I do know something of the life of Marian, for she has been on this earth plane on several occasions: once, the wife of a wealthy Mansfield linen manufacturer; in another, a slave girl in Egypt whose master had lost her in a game of chance to another man and, enraged with jealousy, had killed the man and then Marian, so that she could never speak of the incident.

Marian had also lived a life close to the village of Glastonbury. In this lifetime she had come into the world as a Jew and yet had given up her faith to marry a Christian, a decision that had caused her great difficulties for she loved her husband, John Harrison, very much, but it had caused great alienation from her Jewish family. Much of Marian's life in that incarnation had been spent as a healer, for she had very natural healing abilities and had helped the people in the surrounding villages in that part of Somerset to get by and get better when they didn't have the money to pay for other forms of medicine. Marian had also lived at the time of King Arthur and Merlin, the great magician, and has always influenced me that the great king of yesteryear (and still to come) is no legend but a true story, and that she will always love and help the king the way she loves and helps me.

Marian also lived two lives as a witch, the first as a girl in Wales who acted unwisely and unfairly and used her gifts to help herself much more than others and was eventually hanged. In her last life she had lived in a little village in Shropshire called Chetton, and although not really recognised as a witch she lived out her life as a wise woman, once more helping and guiding the people, collecting herbs and passing on wisdom, something of a fortune-teller but much, much more, even if those that lived in the village did not realise it. I have never really been able to tune in and get too much information about this life and I feel it must have been Marian's last life before her progression to higher work on another level of existence. The only influence she will really give me is of the name Edward or Edwards and of a little cottage and a meadow that was in the area at that time.

Perhaps, as my secondary guide, Marian's real job is to bring the gentle, caring influence to MacDonald's brash, outspoken, matter-of-fact, get-on-with-the-business side. When I make the predictions that shock and amaze people they nearly always come from MacDonald and are given to help me go forward and get people to listen, but when I care or heal or guide a troubled person I always believe it is the influence of Marian that comes through to me.

I cannot really tell you much more about my two main guides because what I have written here is all I really know of them. They seem to me to be two very dear friends who are always there to help and guide me and I feel very lucky to be aware of them and to know them. To those of you who are reading this book out of interest, believe me when I tell you that you also have exactly the same sorts of guides, but you may not have managed to make contact with them or perhaps you have not progressed enough yet to do so. Be assured, however, that they do help, guide and assist you as best they can and they are your real friends. I also think it is important for people to realise that those that help them the most from the other side are those who are family or really love you. If your father or mother or grandparents are in spirit, then often they will come through to offer you advice, perhaps planting a thought in your mind or via a message at a Spiritualist church through a medium. One thing I think it is important to remember is this: when your loved ones first go over to the other side, they don't become all-knowing and full of wisdom; they are much the same as they were in this world and you should treat their advice in that context. Many of us find it hard to accept mom or dad's suggestions whilst living, yet some people seem to think that just because they have passed to spirit they should be guided by their every word.

I hope in the near future to write a book or dictionary of all the angels, with the help of my guides, and if that is to be so I will consider myself honoured indeed, for I have had much communication with regard to angels. Many of my students are so greatly interested and want to know more about what they are and what they do. Indeed, it seems to be a time in the world's history when just about everyone wants to know more of these angelic beings and people are becoming increasingly aware of them and drawn to their existence.

My first awareness of angels came when my mother talked of people having a special guide or guardian angel, if you like, who would be there to help and guide them at all times, but especially when they are in real need. She also often spoke of the great Midland industrialist, Sir Alfred Owen, founder member of the Rubery Owen group, which was situated in Darlaston in the West Midlands, who apparently very much believed in the existence of his guardian angel and told of its intervention and help throughout his life. Indeed, it would seem that he had no doubt that several times it had actually saved his life. I also feel I have been helped similarly and I believe this is applicable to everyone else. As I understand things, although angels are from another existence, they are helping all of us in our everyday lives, however mundane. I have told you in other parts of this book of times in my life when I have been helped in difficult times. I have always been shown the way, so to speak, and my understanding from the influence of my guides is that this is what we know of on Earth as the work of our individual guardian angels and guides.

History tells us much about the work of angels and the Bible tells us of the angelic assistance given to the Israelites in passing through the wilderness and of the channelling of the Ten Commandments to Moses. Apparently, similar occurrences happen to visionaries and seers who today wish to help planet Earth and its people progress and bring forth the word of God. However, I believe they not only bring news of joyful and momentous events like the coming of the Christ child in the town of Bethlehem over 2000 years ago, though some would question that date, they also help people like you and me to make decisions and choose pathways that enable us and others to live and progress in what can be a difficult and material world.

I am aware that much knowledge has been channelled towards me via the guides MacDonald and Marian and through to other individuals within the development and advanced classes of psychic awareness and mediumistic development that I have led over the years. This includes influences such as students being told that meditation and healing are gifts being channelled and influenced towards them by various named angels or guides, but I feel this is natural for those interested in spiritual and healing matters. Indeed, it must be said that those within the medical profession - doctors and nurses, if they would only open themselves up more, would also surely sense the energy of pure kindness that draws close to them in the wonderful work they do.

Some angels are well known to us and, as I understand matters, Gabriel is an angel of the very highest order guarding the pathways of death, resurrection and revelation and, of course, in the Old Testament we are told that Gabriel brought an end to Sodom and Gomorrah. Indeed, Gabriel and the mightiest and most wonderful angel, Michael, are the only angels mentioned by name in the Great Book. It is my understanding that angels make communication between the world of spirit and the beings of Earth possible and for some this is a wonderful experience and it really should be shared by all.

However, my guides inform me that not all angels are good. Lucifer (and the many other names he has come to be known by), for instance, had once been the loveliest and most honoured of angels, yet his own pride and admiration from others, aligned to his mighty powers, led him to fall from grace and ultimately be thrown out of Heaven. For all that, my guides tell me that God loves all and that one day, hopefully, even Lucifer will repent and return to his place alongside the other angels in Heaven. Perhaps we should remember that when we go off the rails occasionally and make mistakes in life that hurt us and others, or decide that we are so important and grand (perhaps self-centred) that we do not need anyone or anything, great mistakes are highly likely to occur. I know that that has been the case in my life and I have learned in recent years to be more modest and ask for help from all concerned, and certainly this is when my guardian angel is very close and never lets me down. The same, of course, applies to you when your guardian or other angels draw close. They will always protect you when they can and try to influence you to do what is right in life. Of course, this is the role of your guides from the spirit world too, who also protect you as a sort of overseer when you are working as a medium or psychic, making sure nothing evil or unpleasant can draw close to your vibration. And your helpers, those loved ones, friends and family, from the other side still pretty well help and advise with opinions and suggestions in the same way they would have done whilst in the body.

I think it was a good idea, as Jeffrey Simmons suggested, for me to give an overview of what these people are for me and for you the reader and I hope it is something you will find beneficial.

Chapter 10

Further Guidance

Let me tell you the story of one of my other guides, Standing Bear, or should I say let me tell you what he says about himself. There are certainly those who would doubt his existence, but he has proven to me time and time again that without a shadow of a doubt he did exist in the past, he does exist in the present and he will exist in the future. This is what he says to me about those who do not believe in him:

"Philip, you will find those who will strive to prove that I do not exist, that I am a figment of your imagination, but have I not given you my proper Indian name, the country of my birth, my tribe and the village that I lived in? But I have also warned you, pass not this information on, as others will say you have read of me in a book and it is false. Those who believe in you, Philip, will also believe in me. Those that wish to listen not and believe not, let them be as passing clouds that move on to allow the sun to shine on those that wish to know more. But truthfully I only have an interest in the words that I offer of wisdom, a message for mankind, and nothing more. I have chosen this pathway and to work with you, Philip, in much the same way as the great Marian and MacDonald have done, and have chosen the pathway that takes me into communication once more with planet Earth. It is part of my own progression to teach and speak to your peers through you the truth of the great White Spirit. You and I together must try to reach the souls of people and bring about a greater understanding of the great White Spirit to the inner psyche of the people who live upon the place of residence that you and they understand only as Earth. We must try to help the people of planet Earth to progress, that is the key word, progression."

Standing Bear himself had lived on this planet as part of the Lakota Sioux tribe and told me that he, like all those of his tribe, were true lovers of nature and that his people would often sit or lie on the ground drawing up the vibrations from Mother Earth into their bodies. Standing Bear had lived many years on planet Earth and was greatly respected by all within his tribe as a man who spoke with wisdom.

Another of my guides is also a man of one of the Native American tribes, who makes himself known to me by the name of Two Feathers, although this was not his Indian name and he does not wish me or others to know of his tribe. However, there is some information that he has told me that I can share with you. He held the position of Medicine Man within the lodges and he acted almost in the way a priest would operate in our world today, performing all kinds of major religious ceremonies that were required by the people of the tribe. In his lifetime on this planet he had the power to tell the future, perform spells, find lost people, horses or other animals, and bring about good weather, and, although it may be difficult for people to accept, Two Feathers had no doubt that when rain was required he had a dance and the words that would certainly bring it. He also insisted that I had this natural ability to bring about rain and I have had some funny experiences that do fit in with the words that he told me.

Many times I have gone to places in the world that have had no rain for many months and have been waiting for it and as soon as I have arrived in the country it has indeed rained. One good example is when I went on holiday with my family to Cyprus some years ago. Cyprus had had no rain for two years and the people were praying and doing all sorts of things to encourage a downpour. On the coach that took us to our hotel the courier told us about this situation and I don't know why but I turned to her and said, "Don't worry, I'll bring rain for you if you really need it." I never thought for a moment that my words would come true, but the next day the heavens opened and it poured! I have had similar experiences in Malta and Egypt.

But let me return to the work of Two Feathers and his time on earth. He tells me that he also had a similar role to a doctor in our society today and had special medicines and treatments for broken bones, those injured in battle and to cure almost every ailment that was known to them. During his time on earth, Two Feathers' spiritual power often came from dreams or the ability to attune himself in a trance-like state to other-worldliness, I suppose in much the same way as I do today. However, in his time he would spend many hours, perhaps days, without food or water, constantly praying for a vision or spirit to come before him, perhaps in the form of an animal, who would give him great understanding and power. As head Medicine Man, others in the tribe respected him as an extremely intelligent, strong and influential person, and many of the other Indians could see his aura, which was large and brightly coloured and clearly showed to the people that he was what he claimed. Two Feathers tells me that those who are in tune and at one with nature and are sensitive can see this in the medicine men or healers that operate today and can also clearly see charlatans for what they are, in much the same way as they did in his time on earth. He also says that he always charged for his services, and for something special it could be as much as a fine pony or many animal pelts to keep him warm and to trade with throughout the winter. He has explained to me that, when I have wished I could do my work entirely without charge, we have to have rewards to operate in a material world. This was so even for this great Medicine Man who had lived in this world many years earlier and it was something I had to understand and accept for myself.

Two Feathers emphasised that in his time any warrior or woman had the ability to enquire of the spirit world for advice or favour so long as they proceeded appropriately and for the good of themselves and others and that they would often be successful, and he tells me that the same applies today. Apparently, as a young man he would stand on a mountain top and blow a small feather into the wind or towards the sun or towards the sound of thunder, and he would also go to secret places such as a high hill or a mountain top and fast for several days, looking for the meaning in his life or his relationship with nature. Sometimes he was very fortunate and when he dreamed the spirits would reveal the secrets of what was to happen in the future for himself and others in the tribe. He left this life on planet Earth at the age of 42, though his understanding of years is different to ours and he was actually much older than that. He was murdered by a young brave from a neighbouring tribe, who speared him through the neck with an arrow shot from a secret position as Two

Feathers sat silently meditating with nature. However, he held no hatred towards this young man, as Two Feathers understood that it was really just that his life on this earth was done and it was time to move on. Indeed, as the young man's life progressed Two Feathers returned and helped him to become a Medicine Man who would be good and kind to his own tribe in the same way he had been to his.

Two Feathers told me that he even watched the funeral ceremony (the equivalent of our burials in the West) and this is what he had to say:

"From high on a mountain top I watched the tribe mourn and celebrate my passing to the higher life. Sweet Water, my companion in life, in her grief had cut off two of her fingers. In a second I felt myself standing at her side but she could not hear or see me. So brave and courageous, her fingers pouring with blood, yet never a tear did she shed, although her heartache was deeper than the river that ran between the mountains. On the seventh day of the celebrations, the warriors carried my rigid body high into the mountains and placed it supported in trees in much the way my forefathers and ancestors had been laid to rest for centuries. The chief of the tribe spoke these words: 'Let the spirit of Two Feathers fly swiftly to that land of the happy hunting grounds and may the Great Spirit receive him with kindness and great spiritual gifts. Our tribe shall not forget you, Two Feathers, and we shall talk in the lodges of you and speak of you with kindness and tell the little ones of your wise ways and your wisdom and may you always be with us in spirit.'

"With those final words the chief threw his arms in the air and the tribe walked back down the mountain towards the village. Women and children cried, some warriors whooped and raised their weapons in salute, others looked to the ground with deep, heavy hearts. For many days and months Sweet Water visited the place where my body lay in the trees and sat and talked to me, always asking the Great Spirit to reunite us once again. Many times I tried to speak and reassure her that one day I would come for her but she could not hear me the way that you do, Philip, until one day, when many, many moons had passed, she came to the side of my tree and as the gentle snow flickered down upon her greying hair, her head fell to one side and she passed to a higher level of existence. Immediately I appeared to her and offered her my hand and she joined me on the second level of existence as you would understand it, Philip. Her body was placed in a tree to the left of mine and many years went by; animals came and claimed our corpses and decomposition returned our bodies to the earth."

As I understand these two Indian guides, Standing Bear always helps me to talk and give advice to those that need it. Two Feathers also gives me wisdom, but also overshadows and influences me when I try to follow the healing pathway. My first experience with these two guides came when I was very small and I dreamed that two Red Indians stood at the side of my bed at a time when I was not very well. The chief, in full headdress, carried a tartan blanket which he passed to Two Feathers, who was not a medicine man at that time but a brave who had two feathers in his hair, to lay upon me. I wasn't at all scared in my dream and upon waking I felt much better and contented, and I have always felt very much at one with these two guides.

But now let me tell you of my greatest guide - perhaps I should say the Guide of all of us. In my present work, at least four nights and sometimes seven nights a week on occasions, I teach and lead development classes for those with inherent spiritual and psychic gifts and generally my work is just to tune in and see that everything is in order for those that would wish to develop. Occasionally, though, I am inclined, or drawn by the higher spiritual world, simply to sit and allow certain students to power towards me. On one occasion I sat with my dear friends David, Wendy, Beatrice, Sue, Jane, Betty and Rita and had the greatest personal experience of what I perceive to be my greatest guide that one could imagine.

In my mind's eye I visualised myself being drawn away from my body into the air at amazing speed until I found myself at a place I can only describe as something similar to Wembley Stadium, yet it was an older building and a place with a more revered nature. There seemed to be hundreds of thousands of people there all peering towards one man standing on what seemed to be a glowing, gold metallic stage. I knew this man represented two things - perfect balance and the wisdom of all - and that he was my teacher and my guide to all that was right. In truth, he was not a man great in stature; indeed, he seemed quite small and very thin with long, flowing hair and - forgive my choice of words - looked to be what today we would describe as a Hippy or New Age-type character and someone we would not imagine in our world would draw great crowds. His eyes, however, which I cannot describe as either brown or blue, pierced my inner soul, and as he raised his finger the multitude that stood around me hushed into silence.

Truly, then, this man must be someone special, I thought. I focused on his face as I would with anyone that I wished to attune to in a psychic way, hoping to tune into his vibration, but the goodness that radiated from him knocked me back. I thought many times that I could attune to perfect balance, but this man was so perfect that it was almost impossible for me to do so and I immediately realised that the only communication that could ever be made would be when he attuned to me! I prayed in my simple form there and then that he would do so and it came into my mind that this could be Jesus.

Most of us have seen a painting or a picture and, indeed, most descriptions probably tend to be vain, but somehow I felt that this was Jesus and that in some way I had been incredibly lucky to be projected, perhaps into a time slip, to hear him speak. On the other hand, perhaps the event was happening in the here and now and I had been lucky enough to be one of the thousands who seemed to have been chosen to hear him. I thought I had just tuned in to what had once been, but suddenly the wonderful being who stood before me stopped speaking and pointed his finger at me and possibly a dozen other people.

"Follow," he said in a soft, gentle voice.

Immediately, the situation as I had perceived it changed. I was no longer in a great stadium, there were no other people and I simply followed behind this man dressed in a simple, plain, red robe and now surrounded by what looked like a beautiful golden halo. He motioned me to sit at a small table, where immediately my guide and friend, Marian, appeared to me and produced a large and beautiful book bound in gold. It had my name upon it and Marian pointed and motioned to me to open it. I turned to look to the figure who had led me there.

"Master …," I said.

He raised his hand to silence me and literally vanished before my eyes.

"Read the book," said Marian. "If you can learn, understand and reach the world, one day you will meet our Master again."

I believed her!

"Marian, was that Jesus?" I asked.

"Read the book," she repeated.

So I opened the pages and there was my name printed in gold lettering. The next page had the heading 'The Story of Your Life' and it gave me much advice that in truth, at this stage, I cannot pass on to you but I will give you some information from it. It basically told me that I should accept my life as it unfolds - the good times, the bad times, the challenges - and that I was making great progress. It also told me I had much work to do.

At this stage I heard two of my best and trusted students, Wendy and David, calling to me and Marian also motioned to me that it was time to return for now. Within seconds I felt myself returning down what I can only describe as a sort of tunnel of amazing swirling lights that supported my body, yet projected it forwards, and then, almost with a jolt, I was back in my seat at the head of the circle. I opened my eyes and could see my students, my friends, but could not speak. I heard words forming in my mind:

"Philip, tonight you were drawn very close to me. It is your reward. But know that you have many tasks to go forward and do for me. All of us in the Light have great battles against the powers of Darkness. This is not evil as you understand it, but the greed and wickedness of men and women and those that influence them so. You have a great part to play, Philip, in the development of the godly light force that must be brought towards earth. Do not be sad. Try to remain in good spirits and know that my love and the force of God are with you. Go forward, speak the words as best you can. We will overshadow and help you at all times. Try to bring to the people an understanding of their purpose in this life and the destiny that beholds them. Teach your brothers and sisters to have love and compassion for their fellow men and women. For love truly changes everything for the better."

I still remained frozen, unable to speak; perhaps a better description would be knocked back by the total perfection and beauty that spoke to me. I know this is a strange thing to say, but at exactly that moment my head swam with the sound of a song by The Hollies, which had been a favourite of my mother's, 'He Ain't Heavy, He's My Brother'. This made me smile and yet feel sad at the same time. For in that split second I thought of the times my mother would use those very words to my daughter Nadine about her little brother. Perhaps he had been naughty or awkward to deal with and mom would always speak of this being the key to us all in this world - getting along together, and here was what I perceived as being the greatest man, perhaps the greatest medium, as mom would often say, who had ever lived, once more reminding me of those very words.

Again he spoke to me: "Awake now, tell this little group of friends of what you have experienced this evening, then go home, go into your meditative state and write in honesty what you think is channelled towards you."

The following day I did just that. Whether it is the rambling words of an imaginative author or a true vision of the greatest man that ever lived I cannot say. I can only say that what I write is the truth as I understand it.

Apparently there are many misinterpretations in our Bible of the man known as Jesus. Indeed, I am led to believe that he lived a very normal existence on our planet and, although a great teacher, he was very discreet and, in truth, very little was recorded of his work. But the work of Jesus was very significant. He came in order to give mankind the chance to change his ways, to be forgiving and understanding of those less able to operate in difficult times, indeed, in a time that had reached an all-time low. Jesus brought the message to Earth from God for all men. Many at that time saw him as a figure of great mystery. Most of the things that were written about him were penned many years after his death and the historians and politicians at that time distorted the truth and, of course, down the years the Bible has been edited and changed according to the views of different kings, queens and religious leaders.

Apparently this was especially so in the time of Christianised Rome, and the places it governed, and by the Roman Emperor, Constantine. But I think you have to understand that it must have been difficult for those who took the words of Jesus Christ to Rome to get a strong hold at that time. Powerful Roman men and women would not easily give up their positions or the life they had understood. Perhaps the emperors and men of great power had to see a way that would lead to them becoming saints or being revered in a similar way. Perhaps the Vestal Virgins would have to take on almost nun-like roles so that they would also remain revered before they would step aside to follow the wise and loving words of Jesus of Nazareth. It is very difficult to explain these things, but perhaps that is the way the institution builders of the early Roman Catholic Church had to present their cause, and as it is channelled to me the Romans would not have accepted the path of Jesus in the way he presented it at that time. Certainly it would have been difficult for the people to have accepted that Jesus was a Rabbi, a Jew, the son of Mary, a Jewess, who married Joseph, who could trace his family back to the original Twelve Tribes of Israel. Even today, surely God must be pained and hurt by the anti-Semitism and hatred that many other faiths have towards Jews. Indeed, even here in the West, at times it seems that we, as mainly Christians, tend to forget that Jesus himself was indeed a Jew and a Rabbi and a leader of those people.

Jesus came to this planet to raise its level of awareness, to bring understanding of pure love being the answer to all problems, rather than perhaps to take away the sins of the world. It seems he will come again, but there will be other beings also and they will raise the level of consciousness of the planet. Jesus taught that God is in each and every one of us, and I believe that. Perhaps you could say that the word God means love and that love creates God and vice versa. Please don't expect me to explain that, though, because these words are channelled to me and even I do not have a complete understanding of them. As I understand it, there are also those who will come and say that they are Jesus or the Messiah or Master, but they are not. They are false. When the real Masters come they will be known by the good deeds they do. As Jesus said: "You shall know them by their works."

As I understand things, Jesus will again be with us along with others and he will be with the first landing (whatever that may mean), and his arrival will happen in such a way that we will immediately recognise him as Jesus of Nazareth. My channelled information also seems to indicate that his arrival will once more be in the place we now call Israel. It is also my understanding that Jesus travelled greatly between the ages of 12 and 27. According to my information, this is the time that he travelled the world bringing balance and knowledge to all its peoples: Egypt, India, England, Japan, indeed, the circumference of the planet, visiting our little island in the company of Joseph of Aramathea and spending much time in what we now know as the counties of the West Midlands and Somerset. I have also sent out my thoughts to the Great One to ask what he thinks of those, like myself, who make predictions about what will happen in the world, the way it must change, what is to be.

What of someone like Nostradamus? Was his work just the work of a fanciful author or did he channel and bring forth the words of a higher order? Michael De Nostradamus made his predictions 400 years ago. As I am given understanding of his work, his predictions were made with the intention of making people change and accept that they are responsible for the world and that they make the changes. I have also asked who he was - was he special? Apparently he was doing the same sort of work that I and others are doing today, trying to bring understanding and spiritual light to a world often influenced by the darkness and evilness of uncaring people and nations.

The darkness has ruled in recent years and only now are we moving towards a new time of enlightenment and light. Mankind should not give up, should not despair, but rather know and believe that goodness will overcome and that love will change everything. Apparently, throughout history there are those that have spoken and predicted and had the understanding of what was to be. This still happens today with people such as myself and others who are attuned to a higher awareness. Sometimes people will say to me that the predictions I make are trivial and silly, that it has no worth to say who will win the World Cup, that this film star will get that part or this or that person will do something that makes headline news, but those are the sorts of predictions that allow me to have the opportunity to speak out and to be listened to by people like you, the readers of this book, and I have no doubt that 400 years ago Nostradamus would have operated in much the same way to start with. Also, unfortunately, we have placed far too much interest in looking at the catastrophes he predicted rather than taking the warnings of his words and changing the world for the better.

Francis Moore, author of the great astrological almanac that is sold throughout the world, was also a very interesting character in history and again connected to me. I once received a letter from a lady at the BBC Studios, Pebble Mill, Birmingham, asking me if I knew that I was a direct descendant of Francis Moore and explaining that he had lived in

Bridgnorth in Shropshire. Obviously, I received similar letters of that nature and they would quickly be thrown in the waste-paper basket, but this letter kept my attention for one reason alone. My mother had often told me of a similar story that we were descendants from a great psychic and astrologer, so this letter led me to travel to the local library in Bridgnorth and investigate the fact. In a large book they had there it clearly stated that at one time Francis Moore, astrologer, had lived at a place called New Barnes in Bridgnorth. So does the blood of old Moore flow in my veins? In truth, it is something that I can neither claim nor disclaim, but I have been told by seven different mediums or psychics that one of my guides is a very famous astrologer and in each and every case he would not give his name to them.

Well there you are, a further chapter about my guides. Be aware that you have them too and that they influence and help you in your life, but also remember that you are guided by one great light, a loving light. For me, that is epitomised by the man we have been taught of as the Nazarene, Jesus, the greatest medium that ever lived, and whom I feel should be considered above all others. I am confident that he will guide me all my life and would suggest that you could find no finer guide either. His way will always mean that peace will be with you.

Chapter 11

A Pilgrim's Progress

The year 1995 saw me paying my regular annual visit to Stonehenge, for no particular reason other than that I like the place and I suppose over the years it has become something of a pilgrimage to me. In mid-June of that year I found it to be particularly busy on the day that I visited. Indeed, two young girls who were standing in front of me in a long line of people treading around the cordoned-off pathway turned back before they even reached the start, stating quite loudly and brashly to all and sundry, "Let's forget it - they're only a load of old rocks! You can't even touch them let alone sit on them and have your photograph taken or carve your initials into them. Let's go back and have an ice cream and see if the gift shop is any better!"

Their comments immediately drew numerous reprimands from those in the long queue who had heard them, including my companion on that day, an eminent doctor, and three New-Age-type youngsters who were very poorly dressed and had their hair matted and plaited in a way similar to many other youngsters that were there that day. One lad in this group shouted after the girls, "You stupid, materialistic morons! Go away." (Or words to that effect!) The two girls in their pretty pink shell suits looked over their shoulders, stuck their noses in the air and walked on.

I suppose in all honesty I too tutted a couple of times and yet, thinking about it, the girls did have a point. If they couldn't touch the wondrous stones, how could they feel a vibration or sense anything that would change them from wishing to carve their initials on the stones to perhaps knowing more of the stones and, indeed, themselves? When I visit sacred places or sites that have been important to our ancestors, I must admit that at times it seems as though there is something not quite right, not as it should be, and as a sensitive I must tune in to these feelings.

I am sure that the experience must be the same for the thousands of visitors to the wonderful old and ancient places that we have in the UK, in that, when they actually get to their chosen destination, tourism has changed it and perhaps they stand, hands on hips, wondering what it's all about! I believe that we have bred a generation that tends to stand and view, look at things from inside a car or, at the very best, walk around the advised or guided tour route. I feel it is fair to say that as a nation we have become detached in some way, accepting views from a distance rather than having a desire to seize the opportunity to touch, sense and feel for ourselves.

I was very lucky really that as a boy and in my teenage years my parents took me to places all over Great Britain and encouraged me to see certain places as a sort of pilgrimage, a visit with a spiritual meaning and where things could be learned. As I have grown into a man I have tried to teach my children and my wife to see things in the same way when we have visited various places around the world. I am not saying that a trip to McDonald's or Burger King isn't fun when you are on holiday, whether in Florida or Wiltshire - it is! But when you visit old and sacred places it is nice to know that there are energies there that can balance and help you to grow as a person spiritually and psychically, if you like. Whenever I travel these days I try to organise my time so that I can visit somewhere special on planet Earth, and I would like to think that this book will encourage you, the reader, to do the same. Let me give you one further piece of advice on that score. If you are driving anywhere, try to walk a little way on the final part of the journey. In my experience, this helps to bring me in balance with the earth beneath my feet and to feel the vibrations of the place and, if it is a special site, such as a collection of standing stones, I always try to walk clockwise around it. This will help you to understand and acknowledge its centrality. When it is time to leave, it is my understanding from my guides that it is not really wrong to take something if you feel it will help you in the future, though I am not suggesting for a minute that you go round chipping pieces off the stones at Stonehenge! For instance, a flower or a little stone that you see before you on the ground is perhaps meant for you and, indeed, you should take it. I'll leave it there and take off my lecturing hat, and tell you now of some of the 'pilgrimages' that I have made in my life.

I shall never forget my visit to the Egyptian pyramids. Their effect on me is quite impossible to explain in a book, but what I can say is that my psychic abilities were definitely heightened and attuned from walking around this amazing example of man's ability to create wonders upon earth. However, my personal journey did not start in far-off Egypt. I believe I have been led to places right here in Britain, or Albion as it was once called in ancient times. Places such as St Michael's Mount near Penzance in Cornwall and other Cornish sites such as Carn Brea and Chapel Porth have all been important to me and have affected me and I do believe I have been guided towards them.

St. Michael's Mount is connected to the mainland by a short causeway and I had to walk to the island when the sea was out, but as I reached the top of the hill that stands so proud, on a personal level my dreams were fulfilled in terms of what a castle should be like - towering, awesome, beautiful, yet aloof in a mystical, magical way that seems to attune your thinking positively towards the spiritual side of things.

I love visiting Cornwall and its many standing stones and sites. It seems to me that they have a magic that enhances and attunes me to other-worldliness as perhaps no other place on earth can do. The one site in Cornwall that has always been especially important to me is a place called the Boscowen-un stone circle, which is situated between the villages of Catchall and St Buryan. I had been told that this place was special some years ago by a friend whom I greatly respect, and the first time I visited it I had to walk across the moors for maybe half a mile from the road that leads to Land's End and I found it quite difficult to find. Indeed, I had almost given up trying to locate the site on that first visit when suddenly there it was right in front of me, a small opening that led to 19 stones or megaliths, four feet high and with a central stone set at an acute angle. "Magnificent!" I said, and my wife and son who had accompanied me on the trek agreed.

There were several young people there on that lovely day in June - New Age travellers, who all smiled and said hello and seemed very friendly, likewise the many mongrel dogs they had with them. In the centre of the circle I noticed that a very different person, who could perhaps be described as a very middle-class lady, was lying spreadeagled on the centre stone, hands pointing up to the sky and eyes closed. A middle-aged man, her husband, accomplice or whatever, totally incorrectly dressed for a trek across the moors in his sharp three-piece suit, stood in one corner fiddling impatiently, first with his tie and then with a rather ornate ivory-handled walking stick that I presume he had used to help him on his journey across the moor. The woman lying on the stone turned to some small New Age children who were playing around her and shushed at them, insisting that they must all be quiet while she balanced herself with nature. I couldn't help myself and immediately spoke out in a loud voice to her, "My dear, if these little children put you out of balance then it's no good you lying on that stone - you've got a lot to learn before you are ready to do anything of that nature!"

In truth she just ignored me, but it seemed to impress the New Age party, with whom we spent a very pleasant half hour or so discussing spirituality, etc. Two of them, named Sapphire and Amber if my memory serves me right, asked me about my books and my work and seemed very interested generally, and it is always like that for me on these types of visits. The Boscowen-un Stones were wonderful, but this great hulk of a lady on the central stone seemed to have spoilt everything. And then these New Age kids turned everything round again and made it a pleasant day. Yes, perhaps that had been an important pilgrimage for me - I think so.

I once also had an interesting experience at the Men-an-Tol, a strange stone shaped rather like a doughnut - four feet high with a hole in the middle that you can crawl through, which is situated on Bossalow Common at St Just. It has a history of mystical, magical abilities to cure people's ailments and the first time I visited this site I had a terrible migraine. My psychic friend and companion insisted that I should crawl through the hole looking towards the sun, and in truth when I did so my headache seemed to lessen. Mind over matter, you might say, but the fact is that it did improve.

The moor that lies between Penzance and St Just has many ancient sites and is rich in the legend that the spirits of ancient Celts abound on the land. I have many friends in Cornwall and it appears to me that they are a people who are naturally very psychic and who from time immemorial, I suppose, have practised magic and revered their wise men and women, whilst other parts of Great Britain and Europe have laughed at them. The neighbouring county of Somerset, and the town of Glastonbury in particular, has always drawn me like a magnet and I am always very pleased to see Glastonbury Tor come into view when I reach that part of the country. At the foot of the Tor lies the Chalice Well, a wonderful source of spring water that has gushed out of the Tor for as long as folk can remember. The first time I visited it I found it to be the most peaceful and balancing place one could ever wish to be.

I am also very interested in ley lines. I first became interested in them after reading a book written by the famous Hereford archaeologist, Alfred Watkins. Indeed, this was an old book that had been written and published in the early 1920s and had been given to me as a Christmas gift from a friend in the antiques business.

Basically, Watkins believed that there were lines or tracks running across the earth that were the remains of very old roads or paths used by people in the long distant past. He claimed that these tracks usually passed through ancient sites, buildings, castles, churches, etc., and as a young man, when I had more time to spend looking for them, I found this to be very true and accurate. If you took out a map and started with something like a castle or a church, you could place a ruler on that map and find it aligned with similar sites, just as Alfred Watkins said they would, and for many years this is exactly what I did.

Indeed, my friends and I discovered that there were ley lines right across Great Britain and the world. We spent a lot of time feeding energy into them, which basically meant standing on the ley lines with crystals in our hands and sending love and positive energy thoughts down towards them, hopefully to balance and make good and remove any negative energy that might be within them. I have often asked my guides to help me with this, but in truth little help has been given; perhaps it is something you have to learn and attune to yourself. Having said that, many of my friends claimed to have been guided and helped and to this day they are planting crystals and working on ley lines all over the world.

Apparently, even such places as the UK's Buckingham Palace and The White House in America lie on strongly energised ley lines that are not perfectly attuned and in balance, and this also applies to the area from which I originate, the West Midlands. I suppose wherever you, the reader, may live, there must also be ley lines that meet, that need energising and balancing out and perhaps you will also be able to help after reading my book. I do feel that in the future I really must try to put more into this work myself and perhaps start my pilgrimages all over again. During the last two or three years I have simply had too many commitments with my work as a demonstrating Spiritualist medium to think about the importance of visiting such places, but my New Year resolution for 2007 was to set a little time aside to make some effort to get to these wonderful places more often once again.

A lesson I think I have learned for myself and you, the reader, could learn from also, is that at times I have tried to see far too many places and things too quickly and have not really given enough time to getting onto their vibration to understand them and know them properly. I think that has been especially true when I have combined this work with a holiday.

My old friend Jim, whom I have mentioned elsewhere, used to say that if you could remember the sixties you hadn't really been part of it, and maybe that also applies to a pilgrimage in life to an important or sacred place. You don't have to video it or film it or remember it, what you have to do is sample it and be part of it at that time. So take your time and enjoy, as they say! For this pilgrim, at least, I think that has equated to spiritual progression in my life. I hope it does for you too.

Chapter 12
Predictions Are My Business

For the last few years I think it would be fair to say that I have become very famous indeed for my ability to make what people in the media have called amazing predictions, and colleagues, friends, fans and those who have got to know me all ask me the same question: "How do you do it, Philip? How is it possible to know that the bones of the Russian Tsars would once more be found and positively identified as being the remains of the Russian royal family?" Or perhaps predictions relating to more trivial matters, such as when I said I expected Joan Collins to swap roles with her sister Jackie and write a best-seller, and I told sports fans that David Beckham's time in Spain was coming to an end and that he was on his way to America, and also to watch out for Victoria getting together with the Spice Girls again.

I think one of the funniest stories relates to the New Year predictions I made in 1992 on BBC radio. I predicted that Lady Helen Windsor would get married and the information that I received on that prediction was so clear that I also put myself right on the spot and said she would go on honeymoon to Greece. A few months later the announcement was made that she was indeed getting married that year but they would be spending their honeymoon in the West Indies. Yes, a lot thought, pretty good but not spot on! However, there was to be a twist in the tale, because right on the eve of their marriage, to avoid publicity and I suppose to stop the newspaper people making their life a misery, the royal lady and her new husband flew to Greece to spend their honeymoon there! I was quite pleased about that because once again I had been proved right, but about a week later I received a letter from the Pebble Mill studios marked for my personal attention and written by a most irate gentleman. It read thus:

"Philip Solomon, you are nothing but a fraud. No one could make a prediction like you have about Lady Helen Windsor and the place she would spend her honeymoon. It is quite clear to me that you obviously have the ear of either members of the royal family or more likely their less loyal, and thoroughly disreputable, servants. If you are that good at making predictions obviously you would win the Lotto competition every week and become a millionaire and not be doing the thoroughly wasteful work you are doing now.
- Signed, Mr Unknown"

It was a shame really, as I would really have liked to write back to 'Mr Unknown' had he put his name and address on his letter, because I certainly did not have prior knowledge of these events and if I had known any of the royals I am absolutely sure they would not have told me any more than they would tell anyone else outside their immediate family about that clever honeymoon alteration that had been arranged by Lady Helen Windsor as she was known at that time. Furthermore, it has always been my belief according to what I have been taught by my family, guides and others that you cannot use your psychic skills to win money or competitions or achieve great material gains for yourself and I don't believe it is possible to win the Lotto using my mediumistic or psychic gifts. It might be possible that if you really needed some money you might be helped to find the winner of a race or something or that money would come your way by some means, but the Lotto draw? I wouldn't think so, and if I ever got anything really wrong prediction-wise it was to do with the lottery.

Going right back to the start of the lottery competition in 1994, I received a telephone call from the editor of the *Sunday Mercury*, Peter Whitehouse, who asked me if I would have a go at predicting some numbers for him for the lottery. "I can't really do that," I told him (basically because of the reasons already given above), "but what I can do is think about some numbers that would be in balance for you."

"Okay," said Peter. "Do that for me and when you've got them let me know what you think. Perhaps you would like to write a little feature about numbers in balance for everyone and come up with some idea of what the numbers might be."

"What are you asking me to do, Peter, predict the lottery?" I laughed.

"Well, you know, it's a bit of fun really isn't it, Philip - see what you can do," he replied.

A couple of weeks later I received a telephone call from a reporter who mentioned my conversation with his boss, Peter Whitehouse, and asked if I would have a go at picking some numbers. I obliged but at the same time wondered whether I was making a mistake in some way.

I was very disappointed to read the Sunday newspaper the following week. The headlines said that I actually thought those numbers would win the lottery. Anyone who knows me or has been aware of my predictions knows that I would never do that. What I had said was that I thought the numbers would be in balance with the machine, and that is basically what I had done with Peter as well - I gave him some numbers that I thought would be in balance with him, nothing more, nothing less!

As you can imagine, I received another letter from 'Mr Unknown' pointing out that I had not picked the winning lottery numbers and if 'Mr Unknown', who seems to have a great interest in my career, happens to be reading this book for any reason, yes, I am aware of that fact and let me tell you here and now that I was misquoted. But I expect that is the case for many psychics - misunderstood, misquoted, highly praised; people always looking to find out what the trick is when we are correct, pilloried when we get some predictions incorrect (which we all do), or when we are misquoted.

Sometimes when we honestly say what is given to us that can also make us a little unpopular. When I predicted the separation of Prince Charles and Princess Diana, many people did not want to accept that the fairy tale would ever end. Also, in 1992, a lot of my Asian colleagues and friends were upset when I predicted bloodshed that year between India and Pakistan, but it was one of the big world stories that year. Also in America I warned of an attack by the end of October 1994 on a leading politician, possibly the President, and although accurate the incident was thankfully less serious than it could have been.

However, there are always two sides to the coin. In 1990 the Duchess of York was a very popular lady. I predicted that year she would give birth to a baby girl, a red-head just like her mom. She did and the nation was very pleased with me, as was the Duchess of York no doubt. I also predicted that year that the Black Country comedian, Lenny Henry, who comes from Dudley from where many of my own family originate, would be in for a very big year involving America. That year he was offered a big film part and did a lot of work in America and I do know on a personal level that Lenny and members of his family were very surprised by the accuracy of that prediction.

As described in more detail later in this book, I predicted UFO sightings over central Birmingham on 18th February 1992, which again proved to be accurate in the view of many West Midlanders who claimed to have seen UFOs and other psychic phenomena that night. Obviously many will claim that it was a self-fulfilling prophecy, but I believe the guides told me to give the world that information. It proved to be true and the rest is history, as they say!

I tend to make a lot of predictions about the royal family and this tends to do two things, either amuse people or make them angry. In 1994 I predicted that the Duchess of York, or Fergie to those of us who like her, would be a big success as a writer. Not many people in the media would accept that, but 1994 saw her start work on the 'Budgie' series of books, which went into publication and became major sellers. She also wrote the 'Brum Motor Car' series for children, which also became a most successful children's television programme. I also predicted a girlfriend for Prince Edward, which, again, those in the know thought very unlikely. But again, I was correct. I also warned that in 1994 there would be talk of divorce for Charles and Diana, which again, unfortunately, proved to be correct. But I also said that this would be a period of achieving new stability for the Queen and that Prince Andrew and Fergie would once again become very good friends, possibly more, and I think it is fair to say the media have proved that prediction to be very accurate indeed. Even to this day, it is claimed that they are still the best of friends.

As a Sun sign astrologer and showbiz character, I often make predictions about sport as well and I warned Lennox Lewis, the heavyweight boxing champion, that he would be in for a very big battle to hang on to his title and that, indeed, the Americans might well rule the roost, and in the event the heavyweight championship was unfortunately to go back across the Atlantic that year. However, I told Frank Bruno that in the future he would do one of two things, either retire or finally become the champion. The accuracy of Frank's prediction pleased me very much, for I know he is a very nice and good man, who in his fourth attempt finally became world heavyweight champion.

That year also saw me make one of those predictions that seem to bring about infamy or fame. I had been on a TV programme with a presenter and good friend of mine, Malcolm Boyden, of BBC Radio WM, and he asked me to give my opinions of the forthcoming World Cup, for example, who would do well, what colour teams would be in balance and harmony, etc.

"I'll do better than that for you, Malcolm," I said. "I will also tell you who will win the competition and what the score will be in the final. It is Brazil's destiny to win the World Cup this year and the score will be 3-2 at the final whistle."

Malcolm looked at me and smiled, "Don't be silly, that's an impossible prediction!"

"Well, I'll stand by it anyway, Malcolm," I answered.

In fact I thought Brazil would meet Germany in the final and the German team should really have reached the final but didn't. However, it is fair to say that it did end up with the result that Brazil got to the final and after extra time and penalties Brazil won the trophy 3-2, and once more the letters flooded in to Pebble Mill and to my own PO Box asking how I did it, whether there was some sort of trick involved and how others could make similar predictions. I must say, if you are prepared to work very hard at it and learn a method of concentration and do a lot of meditation, I feel that lots of other people could make similar predictions. Whether they could make them with the same accuracy as I do, I wouldn't like to say, but I know that some of the very special predictions I make are given to me by my guides, usually MacDonald. Like it or not, you must have the publicity and become a public figure if you are to help and guide others, but you can train your insight to make predictions if that is what you want to do.

Perhaps this would be a good time for me to tell you about the methods I use to focus and meditate. My friends in this world and other worlds taught me that to see things more clearly and spiritually, such as auras, other worlds and the perception of higher beings, I had to learn to open the so-called 'third eye', which is situated just above the physical eyes, in the centre of the forehead, and that I had to undertake an exercise of concentration to develop and fine-tune this method of clearer vision.

I always try to find time and space to dedicate to this process, somewhere that it is clean and peaceful and, in my case, preferably on my own. I usually meditate for about ten minutes over five consecutive days, although sometimes I don't meditate at all for quite long periods. I wear very light, comfortable clothing and go through a simple cleansing exercise of brushing my teeth, washing my hands and, if I have the time, taking a shower. I never drink any alcohol at all at this time and avoid, if at all possible, taking any medicines. I always meditate on an empty stomach but have some food straight after, although the latter is a personal preference and some psychics leave a period of time afterwards before they eat. I also try hard not to be anxious or bad minded in any way, feel any jealousy or have any bad feelings towards anyone. This is always important to me.

What I usually do then is sit cross-legged, hands on my knees, and focus on something such as a flower in a vase or sometimes a particular crystal that I like. I tend to sit very upright and straight-backed and follow a deep-breathing exercise. What I actually do is look straight at the object I have chosen, breathe in deeply through my nose, hold my breath, breathe out, pause for a short time and then repeat the exercise about ten times. When I inhale, I pull my stomach right in and when I exhale I force my stomach out again, always breathing in a steady rhythm. This I generally do for about 30 seconds and then I relax my body for another 30 seconds before returning to a rigid position once more. I then look straight at the object I am focusing on, close my eyes for ten seconds, open them, count to ten, close them again, and then focus again on the object. At this stage I will not blink at all but stare at the object. I then close my eyes and visualise in my mind's eye the object I have put my focus on, its shape, composition, etc., and if it is something like a flower I will try to concentrate on the colours. I then hold that focus for about ten seconds. It all depends very much on how I am feeling that day, but I may well repeat the exercise three or four times. After about 20 minutes I will wind down, relax and for me the exercise is finished. That is all I ever really use to hone my method of concentration.

I usually then pick up a pen and paper or tape recorder and whatever influences I feel I will write down or record. If it is a time when I have to make predictions for a newspaper or if I am going on television or radio later that day, I will take along the influences that come into my mind or that I think will have significance. Just after practising my method of concentration is also the time when, if I am looking for specific answers to questions, I consider myself particularly attuned. I can't say that it is a method that will work for others, as I have friends and colleagues who follow great schedules and use different meditation and focusing techniques, who sit in darkened rooms or open and channel down information from other-worldliness, but for my general work this is basically the only method I will use probably about five days a week and for me it works. On occasions I will meditate on a deeper level, following the same cleansing process as described but rather than specifically focusing to heighten the sensitivity of my third eye I just sit quietly and meditate on different aspects of my life and let my mind examine and analyse whatever my mind is focusing on at that moment. I never allow any negative thoughts to enter my inner mind space while meditating and I always psychically protect myself in a very simple manner, as mentioned earlier, by visualising myself in a spacesuit, one of the old-fashioned types with a goldfish bowl helmet, which nothing can penetrate to harm me, and I always feel safe whilst I am meditating in that way.

Sometimes, if I think there is a negative force or someone who is trying to cause me problems or difficulties in my life, I will use a method to banish them, which to an outsider might seem quite odd. I think of them as an army of enemies - it doesn't really matter if it is one person or a thousand - and I say out loud what I want to happen. For example, I might say, "I wish that you be driven away and that you will leave me alone and not bring me problems." It is always as I wish and it does work!

I suppose those of you reading this chapter must be asking how these meditative techniques can work. As I understand it, it is quite simple really. As an individual I see myself as a being of supreme importance to me in the life I am living now; I am the mightiest and most powerful person in my life and what happens to it. It is important that I think no ill towards others, and I can honestly say that I rarely do, and I only ask for things that are good for myself and those that I care for - in fact, I find it better if I also ask for help and love to be sent to those that are cruel and unfair towards me in life (not any easier for me than anyone else, mind). I know from my own inner understanding and psychic development, and from information given to me by my guides, that nothing evil or of ill-intent can stand against my powers and wishes, and I know what I am about to say next must also sound very odd to you and is rather embarrassing for me, but I usually raise my right hand and index finger and say, "Let it be so."

People also ask me how I come out of these sessions, as they are often described, and really there is no secret method to this because I am always in control anyway and I know I am well protected. I just simply and open my eyes slowly and relax for a few seconds and I know that the session is over.

When I am going to make some very special predictions, such as the New Year media predictions, which some people may wrongly think is very easy for me to do or is just guesswork, I do quite a lot more meditating than normal and practise regularly to attune my focusing technique to a very high level. For instance, in terms of the New Year predictions for the *Sunday Mercury*, leading up to Christmas I would probably be meditating, focusing on and working towards them for six weeks solid, as I feel it is important to put a great deal of effort into it. Predictions are, after all, my business and the people of the West Midlands, London and further afield want to know which team will win the various leagues in the football world, which boxers will be the new world champions, which film stars will be making the news, what will happen to the royal family in the coming year, what will occur on the political front both home and abroad, etc. Although some of these could be considered trivial, I feel guided by the light and being able to make these types of predictions, which others consider astounding, helps me to get people to listen to the more serious things I have to say as well. In all honesty, the revelations I make are probably more the words that are given to me by my guides, MacDonald and Marian, and if this is my spiritual guidance then predictions are my business, and I'll finish with those words that I told you I often use at the end of my meditation or as part of its very being, "Let it be so."

Chapter 13

The Psychic Spiral

As mentioned earlier, for many years I worked regularly for BBC Radio at the Pebble Mill Studios in Birmingham as their astrologer and general psychic consultant. Every week at the radio station I amazed people with the psychic readings I would give them. Basically, I would get people to write in, and they did in their thousands, to request a reading from me. I would go through all the basic astrological information relevant to the particular individual chosen and would then come to a part of the reading that we called the Psychic Snippets, and every week, year after year, I would get everything spot-on. This often included the names of their grandparents, people they had been married to and that had been important in their life, significant numbers, etc. Indeed, I once gave a man the full registration number of a car he had just sold! Although I say it myself, many people would describe me as amazing.

Being new to show business, I needed to push myself to the fore and was somewhat arrogant, some might say very cocky, in my manner in telling the world just how good I was - yes, Philip Solomon, the greatest psychic in the world! It was not a statement I was afraid to make, and week after week I backed it up with the accuracy of my readings. I have to say that whenever I listen to any of those tapes today I am horrified by how big-headed I sound, but it was my way of getting myself noticed and breaking through into the big league of top psychics. Now I have arrived, however, I think people do appreciate the true me, which in all honesty is quite an unassuming and modest man.

I also wrote major features on all areas of the paranormal and the psychic world for the Midlands-based *Sunday Mercury* newspaper, such as local ghosts and hauntings and methods of fortune-telling, together with special features for certain times of the year, such as Halloween and the New Year when, as mentioned in the previous chapter, I made predictions for the year ahead.

In 1992, suddenly, out of the blue, I was presented with another challenge and this was by the station manager at the BBC, Mr Tony Inchley, and the editor of the *Sunday Mercury*, Mr Peter Whitehouse. Basically it went something like this:

"Okay, Philip, you've made some pretty amazing predictions and perhaps no one has come close to you in this type of work, but there is always the question: could it be an illusion, could it be a trick, is it mind-reading or something along those lines?"

I have always made the statement that everyone is psychic and I still believe that today. My view is that anyone can develop these skills and and make similar predictions. Peter Whitehouse, in particular, took me forward on this challenge:

"If everyone is psychic, Philip, why don't the *Sunday Mercury*, the BBC and yourself get together and conduct a live experiment whereby you can prove that to be true. Let us see that the whole of the Midlands can be psychic in some way."

It was quite a challenge but one to which I readily agreed. Little did I know that over 500,000 people would tune in to BBC Radio WM on 28th June at 2.30 p.m., but I was ready for it. The *Sunday Mercury* gave it a very big build-up for three consecutive weeks, encouraging readers to tune in to one of the greatest psychic experiments in the country: "If you do not believe in the psychic world, tune in anyway! Be part of the greatest mind experiment ever undertaken. All you have to do is have the Psychic Spiral in front of you at the right moment - 2.30 p.m. on Sunday, June 28th. Anything might happen. Philip has said the people of the Midlands can do it; now let us prove him right or wrong."

The newspaper coverage had also featured a few of my most recent predictions: Princess Diana's marriage problems and the death of a close relative (her father, the Earl Spencer, died that year); the Conservative Party's election win; Nigel Mansell's return to racing victory and the championship; and Birmingham City's promotion to the second division. I also stated in the first leading feature that on my visiting certain houses, spoons had been known to bend, clocks had started ticking again and glasses had crashed to the floor. The paper clearly stated that I had made mind-blowing claims that everyone could do this and they wanted to see it for themselves.

On the day of the event, the newspaper dedicated a whole central spread to it, outlining just what would happen and printed a huge Psychic spiral, saying: "This is the Psychic Spiral. With it we plan to trap the mind-power of the Midlands and you can be part of it all, at 2.30 p.m. today. The idea is to tune in to the psychic forces of hundreds of thousands of people, all at the very same moment, as an experiment in unseen forces and if you do not believe a word of it then tune in anyway just for the sheer fun of it. One thing you have to do is simply have the spiral at a comfortable distance in front of you, stare into it and try to clear your mind of everything else. So what will happen? The answer is, just about anything is possible. Those staring at the Psychic Spiral might suddenly see the winner of a horse race, they might have insight into the future, cutlery could bend, clocks that are broken or have stopped could start again, objects might move and it might even cure a headache for you."

Right at the bottom of the feature it also said, "We want to hear about what happened. You can either phone Philip direct on the show, which will be on for half an hour after the 2.30 p.m. Psychic Spiral test, the number is 021 432 2000, or you can write to Psychic Spiral at the Sunday Mercury, Colmore Circus, Birmingham, B4 6AZ."

I arrived early at the studio that day and relaxed myself somewhat, having a chat to the presenter of the show, Jenny Wilkes, who by then was quite a good friend, but it has to be said that she was very sceptical about what could be achieved. The show began as normal, playing a few records and talking, until it was time for my astrological rundown of people's star predictions for the coming week. Then, as the moment of the experiment approached, I spoke to the people of the West Midlands, giving them a little talk to relax them and to prepare them to tune in and be ready to focus their concentration on the Psychic Spiral at exactly 2.30 p.m. A fraction earlier some of the technical staff had come into the studio and told us that a record number of people were listening to this particular show, some tuning in from way outside the normal catchment area.

Finally the time arrived and everyone was instructed to concentrate for

30 seconds on the Psychic Spiral, after which I invited people to call in. Wow, what a shock! Immediately the entire phone system at the Pebble Mill Studios was jammed with calls from people who wanted to speak to me. But even more amazing were the letters that flooded in to the *Sunday Mercury* over the next few days. The following week, Pam Thompson, the main feature writer for the paper, decided that another full page would have to be given over to report just what had happened. The report went as follows:

"The Day the Mystic Midlands Went Mad. It was the magical moment the Midlands went psychic and on what just seemed to be another sunny afternoon suddenly things turned very odd indeed. There were visions and premonitions, unexplained cures, broken watches that suddenly ticked into new life, some people just simply suddenly felt happy and full of energy for hours afterwards, and spoons not only bent in people's hands, they bent on their own."

The *Sunday Mercury* admitted that the results were astonishing. Here are just a few examples:

* Helen Smith of Stourbridge, who had a grandmother clock that had not worked for many years, tuned into the Psychic Spiral and the clock immediately started to tick, chimed a few times and now seemed to be working perfectly. It is truly amazing but absolutely true.

* Jamie Humphries, a 14-year-old schoolboy from Brierley Hill, had just finished eating his lunch when he tuned into the Spiral. After 30 seconds the two silver teaspoons he was holding slowly bent backwards. He said he couldn't believe what he was seeing and that it must have been something to do with the Spiral.

* Laura Patel from Wolverhampton found that her broken wristwatch, which had stopped a couple of hours earlier, had started to tick again straight after the experiment and that the tablespoon she was holding had almost bent in half.

* Cindy Kaur from Birmingham was a lady who suffered from a lot of very bad headaches. She claimed that after focusing on the Psychic Spiral they had disappeared. She was adamant that she hadn't taken any tablets or other cures and, interestingly, several weeks later she wrote in to say that the headaches had not returned and she believed that they had gone forever.

* June Depford, a 55-year-old lady from Stechford, Birmingham, had an even more astounding experience. She told the newspaper, "For six months I have had considerable pain from a trapped nerve in my neck. I had to hold my head to ease the pain it was so bad, even just changing a sleeping position badly hurt me. Even the doctors couldn't give me anything to help. I took part in Philip's Psychic Spiral and since then I have had no pain. Thank you Philip Solomon and the *Mercury*."

* Sue Jones from Walsall saw a telephone, bright lights and an aeroplane as she gazed into the Spiral. Seconds after the test finished she received a call from her daughter in Australia saying she was flying home.

* Birmingham smoker, Harry Taylor, used the experiment to give up his 60-a-day habit. He said, "I tried everything, but nothing had ever worked, but after gazing into the Spiral I haven't touched one."

Perhaps even more amazing, and what really actually shook the *Sunday Mercury* editor, Peter Whitehouse, was the experience of one of his own staff, Simone Steverton, a sales development executive at the newspaper, who took part in the experiment without letting Peter know. Unfortunately, as she was sitting in her home she didn't have much of an experience except that she felt a warm glow and felt somewhere else for a short period. When she walked back into work on the following Monday, however, and looked at the big clock in the main office, to her amazement she noticed that it had stopped at 2.40 p.m. and the date on the dial showed Sunday 28th June. She couldn't believe it and was adamant there was nothing wrong with the battery - the clock had worked perfectly for years and nothing had ever gone wrong with it before. It seems that the powers of Solomon had even had an effect on the *Sunday Mercury* building itself!

Hundreds of other readers contacted the newspaper with everything from visions of kangaroos to tunnels, red lights, weddings and bright circles. A Birmingham housewife even reported seeing a row of houses in the centre of the Spiral with red-brick chimney pots and moving very quickly like a train.

In all honesty, I was not at all surprised by the results. I had taken the readers carefully through the 30-second experiment live on the Jenny Wilkes show and had tuned my own psychic powers towards the circle. I was not taken aback that the BBC switchboard was jammed, in fact I had expected that to happen, and I had faith that the test would work. I think the experiment proved to the world that there are many, many people who are sensitive and perceptive, but they have to learn to tune in and focus on something before they can really bring these innate elements to the fore. All I did was help them to tap into and maximise their powers of concentration and psychic ability to the full. Of course, what we were really doing was clearing our minds and meditating together, and this can lead to a feeling of exhilaration, relieved nerves, or aches and pains going away. Of course, I had also used my psychic powers to pull everyone else's energy together to bring about what could be described as psychic phenomena.

Many of the visions that people saw, in my opinion, were typical outcomes of tapping into your sixth sense. As for all the spoon bending and clocks stopping and starting, that isn't at all unusual - it just shows that we all have a hidden energy source which, when correctly controlled, tapped into and focused, can certainly achieve remarkable results. The many bright lights and circles that people saw could have been the result of so many people focusing their energy sources together and that is what I believe happened. I would see myself as just the psychic medium and catalyst that focused and brought everything together on that amazing day in the English Midlands.

Chapter 14
An Outer Space Calling

1992 was a year in which I needed to get noticed and to make people sit up and accept that I had something important to say to them. I was making predictions by then that others were saying were tremendously accurate and it had reached the stage where I was making what some thought were outrageous predictions, and yet they turned out to be completely true, and my fans had started to see these as the norm rather than anything unusual.

As I sat down in 1991 a few weeks before Christmas to draw up my New Year predictions for the *Sunday Mercury*, I must admit that I felt a little disillusioned and fed up with the whole thing really. I went through my usual method of relaxation and meditation, as described earlier, focusing on some flowers in the corner of the room, but couldn't seem to home in on anything in particular. I finally opened my eyes, folded my arms and thought to myself, "It's no good, I've got to attune myself and get something really special."

At that very moment I sensed somewhere in the back of my mind the influence of my old friend and guide MacDonald, who said to me, "Come on, laddie, pick up your pen and get to work."

My response to him was: "Oh, what's the point? Who cares whether this film star or that film star is going to get divorced or get married, or which Midlands team will have success in the football world this season, which boxer is going to win the world title, which political party will lead the field, which individual will have problems, whether the prime minister will resign or if the Queen will have a better year? It all seems trivial and boring. We can get the information across and make it sound interesting and it always comes out accurate, but who really cares, MacDonald? You need something more spectacular than that to prove to people that you've got something to say and I'm just not getting it."

"Okay then, laddie, what really would be spectacular news?"

"Well, I don't really know, MacDonald. You're the guide, aren't you? So you tell me!"

"No, laddie, I've long since left your world behind. You tell me what would make spectacular news in the world today."

"An alien landing at the White House and shaking hands with the President!" I answered churlishly.

"Well now, that's not really going to happen just at the moment, is it, my son? That's not something even likely to happen yet. You couldn't predict that because you know it couldn't be made to happen, although it probably will one day."

"Something like the Roswell incident then, where that spacecraft allegedly landed in Mexico with those beings from outer space. By the way, MacDonald, what was the situation with the Roswell incident? Was it the truth or was it a major hoax?"

Nothing came back for a short period, but then MacDonald spoke and influenced me again. "It wouldn't help you to know about that. There would be no advantages for you. Let others look into that sort of incident and draw their own conclusions. It is part of the Earth's growth that they do really."

"Yes, but that is the sort of thing that would make front-page news, isn't it, MacDonald?"

"All right," he said, "pick up your pen, son."

This I did and immediately my pen started to scribble and I quickly wrote, "New Moon, February 18th. Much psychic phenomena around the world. Flying craft over Birmingham."

I sat back in my chair and looked at what I had written. "No, no, no," I said aloud. "There's no way I'm going to put that in print! If I make a prediction like that and nothing happens I'll be a laughing stock. Rather than being taken seriously I'll be ridiculed."

MacDonald replied, "Laddie, have I ever let you down?"

"No," I answered.

"Make of the information I have given you and include it in your predictions."

So, together with the usual showbiz, sports, political and royalty predictions, I did include it. Then, a couple of days after I had submitted everything to the *Sunday Mercury* I received a phone call from the editor Peter Whitehouse.

"Hello, Phil. Er, I've been looking over your predictions. Very interesting, mate ... but UFOs over Birmingham? Are you serious? Are you sure you want this including in your predictions?"

"Yes, Peter, I feel it is something you should include because I think it will prove to be true."

"All right, Philip, but you've got to be a little more specific than that, haven't you? People are always reporting seeing lights or things that can be explained. What you would really have to do is give an exact evening or day when this will happen."

I'd known Peter for a few years and I could tell from his tone and the vibration I was picking up that he didn't believe for a moment that I could make such a prediction, but if I gave him a specific day it would at least give him quite a feature for one of his reporters to look at.

"February the 18th," I said, remembering what I had written earlier.

"Okay," said Peter. "Anyway, thanks for the work. It looks really good and the cheque is in the post." He put the phone down.

I forgot all about my predictions then until approaching Christmas, which was very pleasant for me that year and I seemed to be having a lot more success with everything I did, especially in the broadcasting field; indeed, so successful that I had to work on New Year's Eve. The station manager, Mr Tony Inchley, who was a very good friend to me, was putting a lot of effort into developing the Asian network in Birmingham and a lad called Jay Patel, who was the main presenter on that station, asked me if I would be his guest on New Year's Eve. This would involve taking calls from people wishing to know what would happen to them in the coming year, talking about a book I had recently written called *Dreamers Psychic Dictionary* and explaining people's dreams, and then, as midnight approached, giving some New Year predictions for the listeners before moving over to Broadcasting House in London at about 11.55 to await the chimes of Big Ben bringing in the New Year.

So, on the night, I went through all the usual predictions, and then Jay asked me for something spectacular.

"Okay," I said. "I think what we are going to see is a lot more peace in the world and I can see Israel and the PLO coming together and sorting something out, a land agreement of some sort perhaps."

Jay's background made him somewhat surprised by that statement, but he said, "Okay, mate, but how about something even more spectacular!"

"All right, what I want your listeners to do is this, Jay. Watch out for a full moon on the 18th of February. Many people will report having seen things and a lot of strange things happening in their life. I have a feeling, in fact I know, Jay, that people are also going to see UFOs on that night."

Jay, for once in his life, was gobsmacked. "Are you serious in what you are saying? That people should look to the stars on that night and they might see a UFO?"

"Yes, I am. Look, Jay, don't put me on the spot. All I'm saying is that people can expect strange things to happen in their life and if they look to the skies anything is possible."

Jay picked up his microphone and said, "Well, what can you say, listeners? What a statement. I don't think you could finish a New Year show on anything higher than that. Philip Solomon, the great Black Country psychic, predicts Brummies will see UFOs!"

That wasn't exactly what I'd said, but that's the way radio people work. He then handed over to Broadcasting House and we both relaxed in our chairs to listen to the sound of Big Ben's chimes telling everyone the New Year was upon us.

Jay shook my hand and wished me a very happy New Year. "Philip, mate, that was brilliant, superb. I don't know how you make these things up. The fans are going mad. What a statement. Honestly, you really are a card," he said.

"Jay, this is a serious prediction I am making!"

"Come on," he answered. "You can't believe that people will see a UFO over Birmingham!"

"I didn't really say that though, did I, Jay? What I said was that people would have a lot of different experiences and for them to look to the skies. Some would see UFOs."

"Well, whatever you said, I've got to give it you, Philip, you always come up with something different and you've certainly made the show interesting tonight. See you, mate."

With that we walked out of Pebble Mill and into the darkness, and I drove the 18 miles home so that I could spend New Year with my own family. I had enjoyed the evening and felt I'd had the opportunity to make quite an important statement that night. In six weeks' time I was to make very big news, not just in Birmingham but also in other parts of the world. It was in Birmingham, though, that it really hit the headlines.

February 18th arrived and a lot of my friends phoned me to say that there did seem to be a funny atmosphere and as the evening approached it seemed to become more so. More and more people were phoning me to tell me that they were having strange sensations and that, basically, there was something in the air! At 9 o'clock that night my telephone rang for the eighteenth time and I subsequently received around another 40 calls from people telling me they had seen things in the vicinity of Birmingham, UFOs if you like, before I decided to leave the phone off the hook. I switched off my mobile phone too and went to bed, believing that something special was about to happen. The next morning at about 9 o'clock I received a call from Fergus Sheppard, who was the senior journalist at that time for the *Birmingham Evening Mail* and a lad I knew quite well.

"Philip, it's amazing. All last night we were taking calls and already this morning many more people have phoned in to say they have seen UFOs. I think we are going to put a little story somewhere in the middle of the paper about it."

"That's very good, Fergus, I'm pleased to hear it. Perhaps you can give me a ring about lunchtime and we can have a chat about it," I replied.

He phoned me back at around 11 o'clock that morning to inform me that the story was going on the front page of the newspaper. And, sure enough, that night on the front page was the heading 'Great Barr Blue Disc UFO Alert' by feature journalists Fergus Sheppard and Edward Stephens, with the following report:

"A bright light which hovered in the sky without sound led to calls from dozens of Midlanders claiming to have seen a UFO. The vast blue disc was witnessed and seen over the Kingstanding and Great Barr area of Birmingham and meant the West Midlands UFO Network was inundated with many calls. Mr John Hurley from the network said they usually took around three calls a year but yesterday he had received forty-eight. One sighting was from former RAF pilot, Mr John Lowndes, of Crescent Road, Great Barr, who reported a big blue disc the size of a football pitch hovering above Aldridge Road in the early hours of yesterday morning. 'It was amazing,' he said. 'It just hovered there for about ten to fifteen seconds. I don't believe in aliens and saw a lot of things while flying for the RAF, but this thing was amazing.' Mr Hurley, representing the West Midlands UFO Network, said he was baffled. A spokesman for Birmingham International Airport said nothing unusual had been seen or heard on the radio but certainly something strange was going on."

The rest of that day and the next I received calls from all over Great Britain and abroad, from friends, reporters and those with an interest in UFOs asking how I had done it. How was it possible to make such a prediction? In all honesty, for once in my life I was rather staggered and short of words. All I could say was that I had predicted it as my guides had told me it would be so and so I had confidence that it would happen. Most of the reporters said they needed more than that and one even asked, "Are you an alien?" That made me laugh greatly, but I had to say quite honestly in answer to his question, "I don't know what I am; I am the same as you, living my life here in an ordinary everyday way."

That day the *Birmingham Post*, another major West Midlands newspaper, did a feature about UFOs that included my story:

"PSYCHIC TRIUMPHS WITH UFOs. Wolverhampton psychic astrologer, Philip Solomon, enjoyed a spectacular triumph this week. Mr Solomon, a regular on BBC Radio WM, told one of its presenters, and the world, on Jay Patel's New Year's Eve show on the station, watch out for a full moon on February the 18th. Many will report appearances of a psychic phenomenon or UFO sightings. Sure enough, yesterday one of our sister papers, the Birmingham Evening Mail, reported on its front page that dozens of Midlanders had that night claimed to have seen a UFO."

Well, I needed front page news and at last I had got it. MacDonald had not let me down. Since that day I have never failed to receive some sort of offer for a show or feature or to do some other work that would provide me with a living and at the same time let other people in show business and in the psychic world know that I had arrived. Whether anyone else has made such a prediction and it has come true I don't really know. At times it seems a very silly sort of prediction to have made and not that very important really, but people are very interested in that sort of thing and the publicity seems to have equated to an outer space calling, so to speak!

Chapter 15
Hypnotism and Sports Psychology

I have always been really interested in hypnotism and sports psychology. It has always seemed to me that sports people could achieve so much more if they only had more belief in themselves. I think a good example of that was when Dr Roger Bannister ran the four-minute mile way back in the early 1950s when it was said that such a feat would be impossible. But once Bannister did it, everyone else seemed to be able to achieve it too. Today, hundreds of people easily run the four-minute mile and even ladies, who are not supposed to be as physically strong as men, get close to it. But then perhaps there's also an element of mind over matter, and when ladies start to do it regularly then many others will too.

There has been lots of publicity in recent years about professional boxers being hypnotised before going into the ring to fight, although I am a little sceptical that this would happen. I don't think the British Boxing Board of Control would agree to it for a start, and I'm not really sure it could be done or that it would actually work. Many people claim that Steve Collins was hypnotised before his two fights with Chris Eubank and that was probably the reason for his victory, having the edge on a mental level. Of course Collins won the fights physically as well, so he beat Eubank both ways. It is also claimed that show-business hypnotist, Paul McKenna, helped Frank Bruno in his fight with Oliver McCall to become heavyweight champion of the world. I must admit, having watched the fight (and I did very closely), in the last couple of rounds Frank Bruno seemed to be operating like a robot and just hanging on in there, but personally I don't think it was hypnotism that achieved his results but rather a combination of good management, the right opponent at the right time, and his own undoubted courage and ability.

I have a lot of friends in professional boxing and one of them is the very well-known professional trainer Ronnie Browne of Dudley. I have assisted and advised him on this matter of hypnotism and sports psychology on many occasions. Ronnie is a very intelligent man and very forward thinking, and he has the ability to understand that a lot of the fights are won outside the ring. Someone like Mohammed Ali, for instance, would look deep into the eyes of Sonny Liston and other fighters and say, "You're going down, man, you're going down," repeating it again and again. Really, I would say that this is a form of hypnosis in two ways: Ali was hypnotising himself, firstly by psyching himself up to go into the ring and fight a big, powerful man; and secondly, by emphasising to Liston and others that there was no way they could win. It is important that you get sports people to visualise themselves winning rather than failing.

I can well remember a big cup tie between Wolverhampton Wanderers and Crystal Palace a couple of seasons ago and again Paul McKenna was said to have been involved in helping the Crystal Palace team. The Wolves team achieved a draw at the ground of the London club, but in the replay they were slaughtered 4-1, and I do believe that was the best I saw Crystal Palace play that season. I had warned Graham Taylor, whom I hope is a friend, to take the matter seriously. Graham assured me he had and that he was well aware of sports psychology, but the fact remains that Crystal Palace did seem to be the better team in that match. They displayed a totally up-for-it attitude and had winning on their mind, whereas Wolves really didn't seem to be a team that believed they could win. Well, Graham, could I have been right in what I told you?

I have done a lot of work with Ronnie Browne's boxers in the past. I think they have to be intelligent and two of the lads I helped to have an understanding of self-hypnosis, sports psychology and the ability to perform to the very best of their ability were Robert Wright and Shaun Cooper, both very intelligent, quality boxers. In fact, Shaun Cooper, as an amateur, had been the National Association of the Boys' Club champion and was never actually beaten as a professional boxer, until he retired from the sport to concentrate on another career. Robert Wright went on to fight for the Commonwealth title and still today operates as a highly respected trainer himself. I think it is fair to say that these people gained an understanding of hypnotism and sports psychology through my advice and tutoring and by using the methods I explained to them, to help them and others in their sporting careers.

Ronnie Browne to this day is a very good friend and we often meet and discuss these matters. He is adamant that self-belief, sports psychology, self-hypnosis, whatever you want to call it, is one of the most important factors in the sport. Obviously, I tend to agree with him and will continue to help whenever I can. I also offered my services free to Chris Eubank for his second fight with Steve Collins, an offer he didn't take up. I think that was unfortunate really, Chris, because if you had I believe you would have beaten Steve Collins and retained your world championship title at the time!

Hypnotism and sports psychology are like everything else in this world: you always make the choices for yourself, live by them and are guided by them, for no one knows you better than yourself and those little voices in the back of your mind guide you towards being the very best you can be at whatever you have chosen to do. I also believe that the mind has a great ability to heal the body and certainly speed up recovery from the types of injuries that professional sportsmen and women get today.

Over the years I have worked with many footballers and athletes. One particular man I worked with on many occasions and who became a very good friend of mine was the then Aston Villa and England footballer, Tony Daley. Tony suffered more than his fair share of injuries, which in many ways meant that he received fewer international honours than his ability deserved. However, he was a highly intelligent man who could appreciate my work as a hypnotist, sports psychologist and healer and understand how the mind could alleviate pain, make you a better player mentally and physically, and even speed up recovery from injury. Tony now works for Wolverhampton Wanderers and is a highly respected member of their management team.

Chapter 16
New York, New York, a Wonderful Town

In June 1999, I visited New York for the first time in my life, mainly to meet up with one of my closest friends, Professor Hans Holzer. It's not that I hadn't been asked to go to the Big Apple before, many who know me well will tell you that I am much happier performing in the halls and theatres of my own country than in the big venues in America. Also, American mediums work much more as channellers than we traditional British mediums. Having said that, I actually loved New York City, so much so that I was very tempted by Hans's suggestion that I should stay there permanently. I just seemed to connect with the people, who seemed to be very taken with me indeed.

By this time I knew Hans very well and had been communicating with him for many years by telephone or letter, but you have to meet this great man to appreciate what a genius he is. His knowledge of the paranormal and afterlife no doubt makes him the world's leading authority. It's a fact that real mediums can be temperamental at the best of times, but while I was over there I found Hans to be a person who understood this and he always managed to help me operate at my mediumistic best at all times. Of course I gave Hans private readings, after which he bestowed on me very high acclaim, privately and publicly, and in fact declared on record that I was the greatest trance medium he had ever worked with.

I also gave a reading to a very nice man called Martin, who at one time had been the personal secretary to the great Irish medium, Eileen Garrett, although I did not know this prior to meeting him. During his reading I gave him the name Janet as a link with a very important lady in spirit. This he readily accepted and later he told me that this was the middle name of

Eileen Garrett herself and was exactly the way she would probably let Martin know it was her coming through. I then gave a link to a lady in spirit for him, and gave her private nickname. Again this was readily accepted, and many other things were passed to me to help me successfully read for Martin. However, just as important to me, I felt I had met another man who had made a very big impression on me, far more than he probably realised at the time.

Shortly after the reading with Martin, I was presented to the Eileen Garrett Foundation at a special evening hosted by Professor Hans Holzer. Whilst there I met a delightful descendant of Eileen Garrett, Lizette, who if I recall correctly was her niece, someone I found charming and most supportive towards me as an English medium and relative stranger to many in New York.

I also met and successfully read for a very nice lady, Rona Cherry, who at one time had been executive editor of *Glamour Magazine*. Of course, I did many other private readings for people, mainly through Hans's personal introduction and recommendation, some of whom had travelled to New York from other parts of America to see me. I would like to take this opportunity to apologise to anyone reading this book whom I was unable to meet due to my incredibly tight schedule.

While I was in America I did a demonstration of clairvoyance at an event organised by two lovely people, Marshall and Kay Lee, who have since become good friends. I simply went from person to person giving them names relevant to their loved ones on the other side, in the English style of mediumship. It seems that those who received this evidence were astounded and very pleased with my work for them. What can I say? I am only as good as the people from the other side inspire me to be, but it is always good to prove that life goes on and that there is no death to be faced for any of us. I suppose it must have helped those New Yorkers just as much as those in the UK who have come to see me in theatres, halls or for private readings as my clients and friends.

I am a great believer in fate placing us where we need to be to progress, and it also reminds us in the physical world that there is more to life than appears at times. I also truly believe that our life is pre-planned for us and that those in the higher realms help to place us on particular pathways to be in places or meet people to help us.

Such a thing was to happen to me right in the heart of New York's Herald Square. Professor Holzer had arranged for me, my wife Kath and our son Paul to stay at the Herald Square Hotel, which was owned by his good friend Abe Puchall. It was also arranged that I would give Abe a private reading. I had never met Abe before, but immediately liked him. During his reading I gave him the names of his father and grandfather, and also told him that a child had come into the world recently, which was all correct, together with lots of other things that were personal to him. Abe was a nice man who clearly understood my work and was able to accept the information I was passing to him.

Suddenly, however, I was inspired to ask Abe what was his connection with Harry Houdini, the great escapologist. Now anyone who knows me will tell you that I just happen to be a massive fan of Harry Houdini. Indeed he and Al Jolson were two of my childhood heroes, rather than Elvis or The Beatles who tended to be the favourites of the other kids of my generation. "Well," said Abe, "actually I am a descendant of Houdini (Ehrich Weiss), he was part of my family." Abe was very surprised that I had linked into him, but in fairness I'd had Ehrich Weiss through many times in the past but I had never expected to speak to one of his direct descendants.

How amazing that out of all the hotels in New York I would end up staying in this one and I would have the opportunity to give a private reading to a relative of one of my childhood heroes and a man I had admired all my life. Fate had once again played its part in putting me in the right place at the right time. I told Abe many other things about Houdini, which of course must remain private, but if you are reading this book Abe, I understand why you gave me the watch with the smiley face and the t-shirt from Coney Island. Be assured they will remain with me forever. I understand the links with them and thank you so very much.

During my New York stay, it was also arranged that I would be interviewed by legendary broadcaster, Joe Franklin, a man greatly admired by all Americans. I enjoyed this interview very much. Joe is so professional and was totally fair in his approach to what can be difficult subjects to discuss: mediumship and the afterlife. He also talked about some of the predictions I had made in the past, such as the Berlin Wall falling long before politics brought about its downfall, and the making of the now historic peace agreement between Israel and the PLO. How wonderful it would be if this could happen again today.

He also asked about a book I had written with Professor Hans Holzer entitled *Beyond Death: Conditions in the Afterlife*, which at that time was flying off the bookshelves quicker than the bookshops could stack them. I could tell that Joe was really interested, rather than just going through the motions as some lesser interviewers might do, and he had really researched my career. It was easy to understand why he had been the man chosen to interview really famous Hollywood stars and, of course, several US presidents. He just puts people perfectly at ease. In the book *Beyond Death*, there were reports of some trance mediumship that had allowed me to communicate with people such as Elvis Presley, Marilyn Monroe and many other major stars of stage and screen, and here before me was the man who had probably known them far better than most. I also felt he knew and respected my work as genuine. Believe you me, I have been interviewed by people who do simply go through the motions or, even worse, treat serious Spiritualist mediums as delusional, foolish or even frauds. Of course, some of them are, but that's another story. Suffice to say, I am not!

After the show Joe phoned me to see if he could come round to see me and meet my wife and son, and I can only say that he was as charming 'off air' as 'on air' and he presented me with the latest copy of his book *Up Late with Joe Franklin*. Since that time I have kept in touch with him and can understand why they call him a broadcasting legend in the United States, but not only that, I think he is a great and genuine guy.

I was also lucky enough to spend a little time visiting the sites and took some time to stop and talk to the native people of New York. In truth, I had been pre-warned that they could be unfriendly and abrupt, but I found this not to be the case at all. Without a shadow of a doubt, to me they were some of the most interesting, warm, friendly, kind and generous people I had met anywhere in the world. I thoroughly enjoyed visiting places such as the Empire State Building, the Statue of Liberty and Ellis Island, to where perhaps many years ago some of my own ancestors would have sailed from England and Ireland to start a new life in what was a country of opportunity in those days.

Too soon my time in New York was finished, but I have no doubt there will be return trips and I have certainly changed my opinions about the biggest city of them all, The Big Apple. Perhaps it is just as Frank Sinatra, another man I greatly admire, sang about it: 'New York, New York, a wonderful town'.

Chapter 17
Making Psychic News

Towards the end of the nineties, everything seemed to be going brilliantly for me. Everybody wanted me to work for them, demonstrate mediumship or take workshops to teach them to be psychics and things of that nature themselves, and I also had my own spot on local radio every week working as the BBC Black Country psychic.

However, something very special and important in my life came along right at the end of 1999. I met a lady called Lyn Guest de Swarte, the editor of *Psychic News*. Lyn had seen some of my writing and had been very complimentary about it, and I must say I really liked Lyn too. I was impressed by her as the editor of that publication and knew that this was someone who was very special. Strangely - coincidences again in my life if you like - *Psychic News* had always been a big favourite of my mother and I even read myself occasionally as a little boy, and of course did so regularly in adulthood. It is the main newspaper for anyone who is interested in Spiritualism and the psychic world generally and is incredibly popular.

As you can imagine, it came as quite a big shock when Lyn asked if I had ever thought of writing for *Psychic News*. My first reaction was that I would be delighted, but I would have to be asked to do so first, wouldn't I? Lyn said, "Well, that's exactly what I'm doing. Why don't you try a column, see how it goes, and we'll have a look at it again in a few weeks." Well, it ended up being a lot more than just a few weeks! It is 2007 now, as I reach the completion of this book, and I am still writing a very popular column in the newspaper every week! But it was Lyn really who came, found me and sourced me for that paper.

A few years later Lyn relinquished her role as editor of *Psychic News*, and a man who has always impressed me as well as my mother, Tony

Ortzen, a former editor of *Psychic News*, took up the reins again. He had been quite involved with people like Doris Stokes and was greatly respected by everyone. I suppose when Tony returned to the newspaper in 2004 people thought there would be a lot of changes and, indeed, quite a few did take place, but I stayed there and my association with *Psychic News* has remained a great pleasure to this day.

Interestingly, *Psychic News* was first established by Maurice Barbanell, a very good friend of someone else who has had made a very big impression on my life, my good friend and mentor, Professor Hans Holzer, so those coincidences are always there with me. I think it is important to remember that *Psychic News* was the first of its kind anywhere in the world and it is a highly respected publication. As such, I feel very honoured to have been able to write for it for the last seven years and hope that I will continue to do so for the next 27 years.

However, the people who read *Psychic News* are an incredibly important aspect, and every week I get literally hundreds of emails and still quite a few letters too from people of all different age groups who really enjoy *Psychic News* generally and my column in particular, which is very pleasing to me.

Another role I have fulfilled for the last three years and continue to do is being the 'Psychic Agony Uncle' for the independent Midlands' *Wolverhampton Express & Star* newspaper which, you might be surprised to hear, has the largest circulation of any evening newspaper in the UK, sometimes reaching 300,000. This is a very special column to me and I really enjoy it. It was brave of the newspaper, at the right time and place, to employ a medium to act as a professional agony uncle. Again, I get a massive response every week from people either writing to me as a regular agony uncle with questions about ordinary situations or often seeking answers relating to Spiritualism and the psychic world.

Someone who was very instrumental in my taking on this role, and who has become a very good friend of mine, was the head reporter at the *Express & Star*, Stella Stokes. She approached me and asked if I would write the column. I suppose initially I wasn't that keen to do it really, because I wondered what kind of response I would get - positive or negative, but Stella was very supportive and insisted that it would be a major success and indeed it has been. I'm sure at times Stella must have been put under pressure by some of her colleagues and the media for investing so much time and energy in supporting me with that particular column and I will always be very grateful to her for doing that, as well as the editor, a very forward thinking and fair man, Adrian Faber.

It was very early in 2001, as mentioned earlier, that I co-wrote my best-selling book, *Beyond Death: Conditions in the Afterlife*, with the Austrian/American parapsychologist and expert on the paranormal world, Professor Hans Holzer, which resulted in my trip to New York and a great deal of media attention in America. It seems really that the last few years of my life have been very much involved in writing in diverse ways to help spread the good news of Spiritualism.

I think I am probably the first medium ever to have been employed by a major newspaper as a Psychic Agony Uncle, and certainly the very successful book I wrote with Hans Holzer was the first time a major parapsychologist had met in the middle ground with a medium to agree about just what is the afterlife.

Something that did cause difficulties at this particular time was that I didn't seem to be in very good health, but I am a great believer that Spirit supports you and and gives you the energy and ability to do the things they want you to do. I have no doubt that all the writing and the successes I have had right up to the present time would not have been achieved without Spirit's help, and I can only finish this chapter by saying that it was Spirit's intention for me to write all the things for *Psychic News*, book publishers and in other printed forms, which I am grateful to have been able to do successfully so far.

Chapter 18
Taking Tea with the Queen

I think probably one of the proudest moments of my life was when I was invited to a Royal Garden Party at Buckingham Palace to meet the Queen in recognition of my charity work. This was in 2003 and it is something of which I will always have very special memories: going down to London with my wife, staying in Victoria, me in my top hat and tails and Kath in a beautiful dress, making our way through the streets of London to Buckingham Palace, then going through those special gates and looking round and seeing so many famous and important people that day.

I thought it was a fantastic honour to be invited to take tea with the Queen and I can never really understand how anyone could turn down any such an award that Her Majesty might bestow on them. I find it quite shocking really, but then I am sure those who are close to me would say that it's because I am such a strong royalist. Again, I think this is something that has been instilled in me throughout my life by my mother, who was a great royalist and had an immense love for her Queen and country. She was also extremely knowledgeable about Tudor history and I think it has rubbed off on me because I am fascinated by history, particularly British history.

People sometimes ask me, in view of the difficulties the royal family have experienced in recent years, whether I have become less of a royalist than I used to be, and in response I have to say that I haven't. Although Her Majesty has had problems with some members of her family, this just seems to be part of modern life in general; young people today in all walks of life are different from those in previous generations. I feel that the Queen should be thoroughly respected and is someone to be admired by everyone. It seems to me that wherever you go in the world many people envy the fact that we have a royal family and wish they had one too.

A lot of people seem to think that I got my invitation to the Queen's Royal Garden Party as a result of my work with Spiritualism, but that isn't really true. It was primarily in recognition of my other efforts in terms of the extensive amount of charity work that I have done throughout most of my life, but particularly over the last 20 to 30 years.

My mother always instilled in me that great interest in history and also great family pride in respect of our own little town in the West Midlands, Willenhall, and in 2003 I was invited to Walsall Local History Centre to write the history of Willenhall, which was subsequently published under the title of *Willenhall: A Town to be Proud of*. It was a project for which I wanted no remuneration and, although it took a good many months' work and far more research than I would ever want to do again, I insisted that all the royalties from book sales should go to charity. It was a very popular book and probably one of the most successful that the History Centre has ever published (and they have produced a lot of books about local history over the years). The complete run of it sold out very quickly and they did very well from it financially. I received a lot of acclaim for writing it and one thing that was particularly pleasing for me was that someone, I presume from the Centre, sent a copy to former prime minister John Major, whose family came originally from Willenhall. They had been publicans, and acrobats of all things, and I received a very nice compliment from Mr Major, who sent me a letter from his offices in London about his family's history in the town.

Another cause very close to my heart and for which I do a lot of work is anything relating to the visually handicapped or blind. I think that you really come to understand and appreciate how difficult life is for blind people when someone close has suffered from visual impairment. A few years earlier my wife had had a very nasty accident in which she had badly injured her right eye. The Wolverhampton Eye Infirmary and the surgeons and everyone else concerned worked very hard and managed to save her eyesight and, although her vision in that eye isn't brilliant, what they did for her was wonderful and I always promised God and Spirit that if she was helped with this I would try to find a way to pay them back.

One of the things I took on board was helping Beacon Centre for the Blind in Sedgley in the West Midlands, a massive organisation that provides employment, guidance and all sorts of opportunities for anyone with a visual impairment, and I did a lot of charity fund-raising for them. I made a rock' n' roll CD for them (as some of you know, I'm a pretty good rock 'n' roll singer) and another CD of some songs that I had written myself, which did well for them too. Also for some reason an idea came to me (I'm sure it must have come from Spirit's influence) to set up a charity auction. By then, I had got to know a lot of famous people through my mediumship and I was able to harness the support of many of them worldwide. My idea was to get them to donate any type of personal item they wished and auction them off. Everyone I approached obliged and it proved incredibly successful.

Perhaps the star prize that was donated was a Fender Stratacaster guitar, signed by Hank Marvin, which raised £5,000 at auction. The pop group Slade donated another guitar, signed by each band member, and that raised thousands of pounds too. Everyone was very supportive. Madonna sent some smaller items, plus a signed copy of her husband's latest book; Tony Blair sent a pen; Sir Jack Hayward donated all Wolves' worn football boots from the last season and one of his own ties; and there were numerous other items from other famous celebrities too. Since then, it has become a very successful annual event, and I have to say that it is something that makes me very proud.

I have been involved in lots of other charity work as well, especially with healing. Although the healing work is something that I have never been too keen to publicise, I think with the help of Spirit I have had some amazing results in helping people. However, even in this book, I am not going to detail my achievements with individuals. Suffice to say, I very rarely turn away people who need healing or ask for my help and I always try to do my best for them, even if it's only by sending distant healing if I cannot physically visit them.

Another project that I think did really well for everyone, and I'm sure must have come to the attention of Her Majesty, relates to the fact that I'm a great lover of Black Country life. Over the last 20 years or so I have made very great efforts to promote Willenhall, where I come from, hence writing the history of Willenhall as mentioned earlier. In the Black Country we have a regional dialect and speak with a very distinct accent; Noddy Holder of Slade is a good example. I found that people would ask me what certain words and phrases meant, and so I decided it would be nice to put a Black Country dictionary on my website, so that anyone in the world could find an explanation of a word or term, on the proviso that they made some kind of donation to a charity of their choice. Lots of people did get in touch to say that they were grateful for the information I had gathered, even television and film companies, and I know that many that are worse off than ourselves have benefited financially from this project.

I should also add that I have never received any remuneration whatsoever for my work over the last seven years for *Psychic News* and also I just receive an expenses-only payment for my weekly column in the *Express & Star*, which I write in traditional Black Country dialect. I think it is important that we try to help each other as much as possible and let others know about the things that we feel are very important and special, and I have tried to do that with Spiritualism.

I suppose I could go on more about the many charity efforts I have made over the years, but I'll stop there. Suffice to say, I feel that the honour of being received at the Queen's Royal Garden Party has made all my efforts worthwhile and it is something that to me was wonderful and I shall never forget it. I shall continue with my charity work, particularly trying to help and raise funds for the visually impaired, and continue to strive to bring Spiritualism to people's attention and provide opportunities to learn and study our way of life. I shall also continue doing as much healing as I possibly can, but without letting it take over my life too much as I know it could. First and foremost I feel that my life is to be dedicated to being a medium really, a role that proves that life goes on and that there is no death, and this is the most important thing in this world to me. It's even more important to me than taking tea with the Queen!

Chapter 19
Difficult Times

In many ways I suppose the early nineties and up to about 2003 were very difficult times for me, because generally I just didn't seem to be feeling very well at all. I had been suffering from a long-term back condition and arthritis, even a bit of a heart condition, together with blood pressure problems and various other ailments that made me feel quite unwell. Despite all this, I still felt that I needed to be doing something and to work for others, especially in the field of Spiritualism. For nine or ten years I had been very lucky to have been employed by Birmingham Adult Education Authority to teach psychic awareness and related subjects to people in the wider West Midlands, and this is a role I continue to do today for Cannock Adult Education Authority in Staffordshire. I don't think any other adult education authority had offered such classes before and they proved very successful. Many of those who attended these classes actually went on to become quite successful mediums themselves. Indeed, one of the people who became a good friend, John Routley, became president of a Birmingham Spiritualist church and occasionally supported me at major theatre and hall shows.

It was also John who, in 2004, talked me into doing mediumship demonstrations again, because I had become what you might call semi-retired in the field and was finding it much easier just to concentrate on and express myself in my writing and work on my website. It wasn't so much that I didn't want to demonstrate my mediumship at different places every week, it was just that I didn't feel well enough to do it at that time. I also had my teaching commitments and this was something I particularly enjoyed, helping to develop other people's latent psychic abilities.

However, all good things come to an end as they say, and after conducting this training for Birmingham for quite some years the local authority decided they were going to cut back on some of the classes and take things in a different direction. They also wanted me to go on a teacher training course to become a qualified teacher, but I had made the decision that I didn't want to make that commitment. I wasn't in the best of health and I didn't want to be doing quite so much work as I had been doing anyway. To be honest, at times I felt so ill - sometimes finding it hard to walk more than about 20 or 30 yards and in constant pain, that I started to wonder how much longer I was going to be in this world. I still suffer a lot of pain to this day, but I have no doubt that Spirit gave me the healing I needed and helped to put me on the pathway that they wanted me to follow, one that I would have considered quite impossible a couple of years earlier.

It was also a time of great family difficulties too. My cousin's son, Stephen, at only four years of age suffered terrible brain tumours and passed over. I often wonder why it is, that no matter how hard you try and whatever healing is given, whether spiritually or by our wonderful doctors and nurses, such lovely little angels sometimes have to be lost to this world. Maybe it is one of those mysteries that none of us understands, but even for a medium it is difficult to deal with.

My wife's family had to face something very difficult as well in 2001, when our niece Rosemarie, Kath's brother's daughter, who was only 16 years of age, was murdered in Birmingham whilst sunbathing in Centenary Square. I am sure many of you must have read of this incident in the newspapers, and it was a very great tragedy - a young girl, who seemed to have everything before her, snatched away by a madman's knife. To their very great credit, Sean and Karen, her parents, have made wonderful efforts to turn something so terribly negative into something positive by raising many thousands of pounds and setting up an organisation in memory of Rosemarie called Rosie's Helping Hands. A dreadful day such as that could never be forgotten, but it was particularly significant because my wife had arranged for us to go on a holiday to Kenya as an early celebration of my 50th birthday. The day before we were due to fly out, a policeman came to the door to inform us that our niece had been killed. Obviously, we did not make that journey so that Kath could be close to her brother and we were on hand to offer what support we could at such a tragic time. If we had actually been in Africa at the time, it would have been very difficult for anyone to contact us and inform us of Rosemarie's death, as various trips and safaris had been arranged in advance.

John Routley, the man I trained as a medium in Birmingham, contacted me and asked if I would consider doing some teaching for him and appear on one or two shows. Basically, in his words, he told me that he thought I was the greatest medium he had ever seen and just felt he had to get me out of semi-retirement. He felt that some of the mediums that worked at churches, theatres and other events were not of a very good standard and people needed proof that death is not the end and life goes on. Well, John did get me to do a few things for him and I did start to demonstrate at the Spiritualist churches again and then started to do a few big events. The strange thing was, for some reason best known to Spirit, in many ways my health greatly improved. 'Touch wood' is my motto for the year 2007. I have to say that, although I am not in the very best of health, I do feel so much better and it would seem that Spirit intends me to do a lot more work yet, not only in the near future, but for the long term too. The first few years of the New Millennium had certainly proved to be difficult but, as with all trials in life, you have to come through them and move on, and things are starting to look much better now.

By now, of course, there have also been additions to the family. My daughter Nadine married Dean and at the time of writing I have two lovely grandchildren, Liam who is now seven and Elise who is four. I think in many ways having grandchildren changes you greatly. It is absolutely wonderful to see them and enjoy all the pleasures that children bring, but then of course hand them back to their parents when the time is right and continue with the other things that are important in your life too.

My daughter is a qualified nurse but she does to some extent also carry on in the family tradition, as she is a qualified aromatherapist and Reiki healer, and I do feel that finally she is developing the gift of mediumship too. My son Paul works for a company that fits furniture in show homes, and I don't think there is anyone who loves his job or the people he works for more than he. However, he and his friends are interested in psychic things too, and I feel that one day Paul will also bring his natural healing abilities to the fore, for I have no doubt he has this gift if he chooses to use it and I am sure he will in the future.

2007 still sees my wife, Kath, typing up my manuscripts, booking me into theatres, rooms and Spiritualist churches, and shouldering the onerous task of deciding which members of the general public I can and cannot see - a most difficult role indeed! As for myself, I continue to write and broadcast and, in more recent years, have also become a film-maker and director (I have a BA Hons in Video and Film Production). However, most important of all must be demonstrating my mediumship and my ability to prove to others that there is no death and that their loved ones go on forever. Basically I just continue to be guided by the light, and I think I always shall!

Chapter 20

Famous Last Words

I am frequently asked as a well-known medium to operate on a clairvoyant and clairaudient level in order to make contact with loved ones that have passed over to the other side, and to be honest my initial response can cause disappointment. I have to explain that I cannot contact anyone on the other side - contact always has to be from them, generally through a medium, of course. Also I believe that the spirit that leaves the body doesn't just go on to another spirit world and stay there forever. I believe that it progresses and goes on to either higher levels of existence or in many cases, after an appropriate period of time, returns to this earth plane for further experiences and to learn further lessons before progressing.

However, when we first die we do of course pass over to this spirit world that so many people speak of and we often spend somewhere between 50 and 100 years there. My role as a medium is to operate as a channel between the two worlds, and if an individual wishes to make contact with one of their loved ones in our world through me then that is possible, but I must stress that neither I nor any other medium in my opinion can make individual contact with the spirit of someone they would singularly choose. Having said that, it is amazing how often, when someone comes to you very upset and sad about the loss of someone, that very person from the spirit world will come through to assure them that they are okay, that they continue to exist and, 99 times out of 100, that they are very happy and wish those they have left behind not to be sad. I would also like to say to the readers of this book: please be assured that those on the higher level of existence above this life do try to help and guide you and make your life a little easier when they can; you don't need a medium for that, they do it anyway.

I have made contact with Spirit beings in such great numbers over so many years that to catalogue all my experiences would be a book on its own, but perhaps in one way I am a little different from many other mediums in that I always seem to be used as a channel by those that have been famous or were celebrities during their time on this earth plane. At one time I wondered why that was so and whether perhaps it was just due to a vivid imagination. I believe it is important to be honest with yourself and challenge and question yourself in that way before going ahead and claiming that you have contacted people who were probably heroes of yours anyway, but my associations with the celebrity world have been long-standing, so perhaps it's not so strange after all.

I have already told you that as a baby I was pushed in a pram to rock 'n' roll hops by my mother and my father operated as a dance hall promoter and met all the people involved in that business. Later on in my life I worked for the BBC as their psychic, medium and astrologer, and of course this meant that I met celebrities almost every week and many of them booked me for private sittings or we just became friends over the years. Perhaps these connections explain why I am one of the main mediums that celebrities in the other world have chosen to make contact with and use to pass on snippets of information about themselves to their fans. Sometimes these messages come through via trance mediumship in voices similar to those of the celebrities, sometimes with strange accents, and yet at other times simply in my own voice. Here are some examples of the messages that I have received from those we would call celebrities.

Let's start with Marilyn Monroe, or maybe I should really call her Norma Jean because that is always the persona that would communicate with me. Norma Jean made it very clear to me that she was quite happy now and had finally found peace. She also made it very clear that she wasn't happy with the way her money was being spent. Much money was still being made from her pictures, photographs and films and it was going to people she would not wish to have it. Norma spoke of many little children being terminated in her own life on earth and she would much sooner see the money going towards helping orphans or the children in need in this world. She also made it very clear that many lies had been told about her passing to the higher life.

"I want people to stop saying I committed suicide because I did not. I had been sad about an affair that couldn't be and I just wanted a good night's sleep - I did not commit suicide. But don't worry about that, it's done and dusted. I'm glad to be away from the glare of the media and to have finally found peace, but I am glad that my pictures and films and all that material gave people pleasure. I never really wanted to be a sex symbol. I wanted to be a good actress and I tried hard but people never gave me a chance. I also wanted to show love to everyone, perhaps that's why I made so many mistakes of falling in and out of love, but that's the sort of person I was and I don't regret it.

"I've really grown up a lot since I arrived on this side. I'm not a little girl lost any more. I am a strong, intelligent woman, but there again perhaps I always was. But I would like to tell all my fans this, Philip: don't listen to what people tell you about me and do love each other; it's what makes the world go round. My life here is fine and if I say so myself I'm still a star!" [A typical Marilyn giggle erupted!] "When my time comes to progress and I perhaps come back again, maybe I'll be a film director or something." [More giggles.] "Don't forget, Philip, you tell them I didn't commit suicide and tell them down there not to do it either. It's not the answer to anything. Life's for living. Bye!"

I am not given to sitting in gimmicky Halloween show-business-type seances to try to make contact with those that have passed over, but in truth on one 31st October several years ago I did agree to join a collection of magicians and so-called psychics who intended to try to make contact with the former great escapologist, Houdini, a man who always claimed that if there was a way back from beyond the grave he would find it and put in an appearance on Halloween, a day that always held a special significance for him throughout his life, and pass on a secret message relevant to one person in America. This would prove beyond doubt that life after death existed.

In all honesty, my evening with the magicians' group proved a complete waste of time, as it basically went along the lines of individuals showing how they could perform tricks similar to effects that are demonstrated by some genuine and, unfortunately, some false psychics - elevation, spoon-bending, mind-reading, etc. - all very clever but at the end of the day they were only performing tricks that were neither psychic or spiritual at all! Later that evening we all sat in a circle in a small room and one of the gentlemen present turned out the lights and invited the great Houdini to join us. We sat very quietly and intently for about 10 to 15 minutes but, unfortunately, nothing happened. He switched the lights back on and it was decided that for that year they had not been successful in their efforts, but they agreed to meet at the same time, same place, the following Halloween to try again.

For me that seemed to be the end of the story, as I certainly had no intention of joining these gentlemen the following year and didn't want anything more to do with it. However, that night driving home a strange feeling came over me and I just had to pull my car over and sit quietly for a few moments. As I did so, the following words came into my mind as if spoken to me, "I am Houdini, Philip. Ehrich Weiss is my name. In a New York bank vault there is a drawing of a veil and handcuffs. No one alive now is aware of this fact, but it is the truth, Philip. The veil represents the veil that is between the two worlds. The handcuffs are simply the shackles that have been broken by the great Houdini."

"Why have you not passed on this information before?" I asked him.

"I have," he answered. "Twice I have got through with this information, but both times the connectees have not passed it on because they were scared that people would laugh at them and not believe. It is important that people know we do not die but that we pass over to the higher levels of existence and there is no death, only another level of existence."

Houdini also told me that many people had reported that he had spent a large part of his life investigating and proving mediums to be fraudulent. He said that he would like the world to know that many mediums he investigated during his time on earth were entirely genuine. For goodness gracious sake, why else would he promise to find a way to return from the dead? That was all Houdini said to me - not another word - on that occasion.

So please, if any manager of a New York bank, past or present, has knowledge of such a drawing and would like to contact me, I would love to hear from them, but not to prove that Harry Houdini was the greatest magician that ever lived, although I for one believe he was and much more, or to prove that I was lucky enough to make contact with him, because that is not so important either. What would be wonderful is that if after all these years it could be proved that life does go on and there is a way back if you truly wish to prove to others that there is life after death. Houdini, it would seem, genuinely had such a wish.

Another difficult message to pass on came through to me from Earl Mountbatten of Burma, who wished to make contact with Prince Philip, or if possible his favourite nephew, Prince Charles. The earl was murdered by terrorists in Ireland when a bomb exploded on his boat in 1979. The earl communicated to me just before the funeral of the Japanese emperor, Hirohito. The media had indicated that either Prince Philip or Prince Charles would attend the funeral of the Japanese emperor. However, so many British soldiers had suffered such terrible atrocities at the hands of the Japanese that many people felt it was unwise for either of the princes to attend the funeral, and perhaps for those that had served there it was understandable that they would not wish them to do so.

My own father, as a young soldier of 18, had fought the Japanese in Burma and had been involved in some of the most intense fighting in an area known as the Admin Box. I well remember him telling me they had been cut off for quite some time in the jungle and that the officer in charge had told the men that if they surrendered he would shoot them himself, for as they were members of a crack regiment of paratroopers the Japanese would torture them beyond belief. That band of British soldiers had hung on in the Admin Box and basically held off the Japanese army. The battle left my father in a terrible state and disabled really for the rest of his life.

I well remember a colleague of his, a man called Jimmy Bateman, telling me how brave my father had been. Apparently Mr Bateman was part of the greater army that was following up and trying to reach the area of the Admin Box and another of those strange coincidences that often seem to happen in our family occurred again there. Mr Bateman was from Bilston, the very same town that my father was from, and he was the man who found my father whom he described as nothing but a bag of bones, very ill, and with 11 of his comrades dead in a hole, yet my father was still alive at the top of the hole hanging on to a machine gun. Mr Bateman quickly informed the medics that he was still alive, and as he looked over the brow of the hill he saw literally thousands of Japanese soldiers lying dead.

Perhaps it is hard to understand, but my dad is a wonderful man in many ways and never really holds a grudge against the Japanese. He never joins in any of the marches and I can't ever remember him saying many bad things about them. Thus I believe that if Earl Mountbatten did wish to communicate through someone, as the son of a man who had shared the same horrors in Burma perhaps I was an understandable choice. This is what he had to say to Prince Philip and Prince Charles:

"Concerning the funeral of the Japanese Emperor Hirohito, I must inform you that I appreciate that the family within its status has a duty to the public and the leaders of the world to be in attendance. I for one, however, feel required to state that after great consideration and mind searching, I would urge you to send a lesser official, or government officer perhaps, to take your place. Be assured that you are often in my mind and you, Charles, are never very far from my thoughts, but of course you are aware of that."

This, basically, was the message he wished to send, that in his opinion at that time it was not right for a British royal to attend the funeral of such a man. All I could do was get a message passed on to the princes as best I could through a friendly source, and this I did. However, Prince Philip did decide to attend the funeral. Perhaps the message was never received, or perhaps Prince Philip, being the honourable man he is, believed that it was a decision that only he or the government should make. If that was the case, then I for one thoroughly respect his decision. Further communication makes it clear to me that Lord Louis also had the same respect for any decision that Prince Philip or Prince Charles came to.

Elvis Presley has also frequently made himself known to me and those that have sat with me. Indeed, upon returning to the normal levels of consciousness if there has been a tape recorder present I have always been the first one to get my hands on it and listen to the tape as, although Elvis still loves to sing and influences me thus, at times I feel I hardly do him justice. Perhaps more importantly, though, here are a few points that Elvis Presley has wished to be made known to his many followers in this world.

Firstly, much of what we have been told about his death is not in fact the truth. Many people have blackened his name, talking of his greed and drug abuse. Elvis tells me that if you speak to those who really knew him they will tell you that he hated drugs and the only thing he ever took of that nature was prescribed for him by his doctor. He also tells me that throughout his life he had problems with pains in his chest and palpitations of the heart; even when he was a little boy there had been times when he had got out of breath and would rush to his beloved mother for comfort. It was an intermittent complaint really and one that, because he had been such a vigorous, physical man, people had never been aware of.

He was also very upset that people had at times painted him as cruel, spoilt and ungodly. And yet, if you look deeper into the record he leaves behind, you will see that he was incredibly generous to many people. He told me that he paid for thousands of dollars worth of treatment for the dog of someone he hardly knew, and also spoke of the time he went into a showroom and saw a poor black lady looking at a Cadillac and bought it for her. Apparently these are stories that are not known about and he would like to put the record straight.

He also told me that although he enjoyed singing rock 'n' roll, those that really knew him would confirm that his true source of enjoyment was singing the black spirituals he had learned as a little boy on his mother's knee. He also told me that on his gravestone his middle name is spelt incorrectly and that this is a deliberate mistake and has meaning for those that would look deeper. He said that he is very happy within himself and it is wonderful to be reunited with his mother and his twin brother, and although his hair is still black, his twin has blond hair; well, grey to tell the truth! [A little chuckle.]

Elvis is also very concerned about his beloved daughter, Lisa-Marie, and says there are those who have kept money from her: "What is hers is hers and she should get it all." He was not happy about her marriages, particularly the one to Michael Jackson. "I never had a racist bone in my body, the princess knows that, and I respected black people, but being brought up in the South, I don't think inter-marriages work." He was pleased that Lisa-Marie was singing and making a career for herself in that field. He told me he used to listen to her when she was a little girl and that even then she could sing beautifully.

He also told me that he still truly loves his former wife Priscilla and wished to give her this message: "Forgiveness is a two-way thing and I know now what you meant about freedom. Not to be free means you are dead." I asked Elvis what he meant by that, but he wouldn't tell me, saying that Priscilla would understand and he hoped that one day they would be reunited again. King and Queen were the words he used. He also urged her to understand the little princess (I presume this refers to Lisa-Marie, but again I cannot say for sure).

Elvis also asked me to tell the world that people like him, rock stars, are very special people who were sent to planet Earth with a special task in life. They don't always realise it or become aware that they are. It is not simply how much ability you have or how good you are that puts you in the public eye, it is something more, something special. Elvis also had a final special message for his many fans in England: "People tell you that I never came to Great Britain, it's not true, I did - twice!" Elvis also said that his story is not finished there. He also spoke of being concerned about people using Lisa-Marie to forward their own cause: "Tell the princess to do what her daddy would, do your own thing, darling!"

I have also had the honour of channelling the words of John Lennon on many occasions. John rarely spoke of his death, insisting that it was a time in his life that was there, had to be, was done, and that was the end of it, and he held no grudge against the man who had taken his life away. His immediate concern had only been about what would happen to Yoko and Shaun. He thought that Shaun, in particular, would have a difficult time in his teenage years, not having the same musical ability as his elder half-brother, Julian, but would be blessed with a great artistic gift that could easily stay undiscovered, and yet he felt that Yoko would recognise it, despite his outward show of rebelliousness towards those he really cared for.

John often spoke of channelled music and hummed songs to me, but I found it difficult to understand the structure of the music, and in all honesty much of his communication would often be comical and frivolous, when in truth I would always have expected communication with someone like Lennon to be high-powered, high-brow and intellectual. A favourite saying of his was: "What you want, Whack, is a Brandy Alexander and a Chow Mein!" Yet at other times I do feel he has helped me as a person. In his time on this plane, John had shared with me a great interest in the world's religions and had guided me to look into the world of the Hari Krishna movement, a movement full of good young people with kind, scientific minds, who have so many good things to teach the world. Perhaps it is fair to say that neither John nor I are what

163

you could call devotees; perhaps honorary members would be a good description!

I suppose it's natural when communicating with someone like John Lennon to expect the subject of the Beatles to come up, and yet John has shown very little interest in talking about that side of things, saying that he gave everything to the band in life and that it has very little significance to him now.

"Yoko was the way, the light if you like, for me. I found my light, what more can you say? The best thing about the Beatles was the song 'All You Need is Love'. Yeah, that was about the best of it," said John. "But me and Yoko and 'Give Peace a Chance' meant more. People used to think that I wrote things for them, that it had meaning for them. In truth I wrote for me and at the very outside for Yoko or maybe Shaun. That's why I'm trying to get some music through to you now, Philip. You've still got a chance, man. I know you are a good singer and musician yourself. People like you or Yoko have still got a chance. It's not the music, it's not the words - you can sing or say anything - it has a vibration that communicates. Even with the Beatles, there was a message, a hidden vibration, the songs meant nothing." And that basically was the way communications generally went with John.

I also once communicated with Brian Jones of the Rolling Stones. Just on one occasion Brian got through and wanted me to let certain people know that he hadn't committed suicide, he had felt unwell and found himself in the water. Brian's message was a little garbled at times but he went on to suggest that some sort of fight had occurred and, whether accidental or intentional, someone in the pool had killed him. Brian never made any other contact apart from this, basically to tell me to pass on to his friends that he had quickly progressed on to higher levels and would perhaps choose to come back in some other life. He also said that he would communicate again in the year 2009 with a much more clearly outlined story in terms of what had happened to him in the final moments of his life. I hope he does. If there is some closure still needed about what happened to him this can sometimes cause difficulties in an individual's progression and Brian's words to me were at times difficult to understand and explain to others, but I have done my best so far.

I also remember having just the one communication with Earl Spencer, father of Princess Diana, and this was surprising really because it was very shortly after his death. Usually it is very hard for the spirit to get through so quickly and his voice was very weak as I received it. The message he had was for Princess Diana, and it was that she should carry on doing her duty the way she had promised him she would and not do what she wanted to do now that her father was gone. Again, as best I could I got that message to the Princess. It was the only communication I had from her father and what it really meant I couldn't say. I don't even know whether she heeded the warning! Perhaps one day I will be lucky enough to know the answer to that question with a communication from Princess Diana herself.

Another very quick communication also came from the former First Lady of America, Jacqueline Kennedy Onassis, again shortly after her death. Surprisingly, though, this was not a weak connection at all. I never met Jackie in the body, but she must have been a very strong lady, especially to get through as strongly as she did, basically to communicate that she was reunited with Jack (Jack presumably being the former president, John F. Kennedy). Jackie wanted me to inform certain people that some secret papers had fallen into the hands of an unscrupulous former associate, who could damage the Kennedy name at some future time. She was particularly concerned, as both she and the former president felt that at some time in the future one of the Kennedy family would once more become president, and however far in the future this was, those papers could be damaging.

I wouldn't want you to think that all communications are of this nature. They can be depressing, unpleasant or run-of-the-mill, but sometimes you can find yourself drawn to something or someone that you wouldn't like to know in the body. One evening I felt very certain that I was being drawn to the presence of someone very unpleasant, and although he would not give his name I am sure I had been drawn close to the vibration of the former German führer, Adolf Hitler. It seemed that he was not sorry for what had happened or for what he had done; indeed, he believed that the time was right for Fascism to rear its head once more. That was one communication that I was very glad to put to one side.

One of my more pleasant contacts included communicating with the former comedian, Larry Grayson, who basically came back to ask me to pass on a message to a very good friend of his who had handled most of his funeral arrangements. He just wanted me to thank this person for everything he had done, but to tell him to watch his back and have another go at chasing up a business acquaintance or someone of that nature, who hadn't exactly played fair money-wise. He also wanted me to pass on his personal thanks to a couple in Wales who had adopted his poodle, William, whom Larry had loved very much in his life. Apparently this poodle has now also passed away and is with Larry on the higher level of existence.

Perhaps the most wonderful mind I have ever had the honour to channel is that of the great Indian leader, Ghandi. It would appear from the things he has told me, and from the words of my guides and other Spirit beings, that the Mahatma truly was one of those special beings that is sent to this world to guide us in peace and love. Even now, as he progresses higher and higher towards ultimate oneness with the Godhead, the Mahatma sends the message of peace, love and harmony throughout the world.

His message is: "I starved myself to stop the fighting. I deprived my family so that you would have sympathy for those that have less than you. I died in violence so that you would see that violence breeds violence and only peace and love can find the answer to the problems in your world. A disagreement, whether it be between man and wife, nation against nation, or within your own inner being, is useless. Only love, understanding and a perfect inner balance can raise you to a higher standard of awareness."

Of course in this chapter I have only told you, the readers, of a few messages or psychic snippets or whatever you might call them, from very famous people to give an interesting insight into what can come through from those in the other world. But it is exactly the same type of information from the other side that I would pass on to everyday, ordinary people on a one-to-one basis when giving a private reading. I know these famous people will not mind me speaking of their communications in order to give you examples of how we can prove the existence of life after death and other-worldliness, especially to people who are only interested in, or wishing for comfort, from those that they have loved and lost.

Most of my work at the present time involves visiting theatres and halls up and down the country to demonstrate mediumship to quite large groups. I try to make this a show where all are welcome, even the sceptics or those who are dragged along for the night by partners who believe in mediumship, and quite often these are the ones to whom I am inspired by Spirit to give a message as positive proof through my mediumship of a life hereafter. Perhaps this is because they need it the most rather than those who already believe.

I sometimes do a bit of singing at the start and end of my shows and I generally have a good support medium before my main demonstration. A gentleman who often fulfils this role is my good friend, the Birmingham medium John Routley, whom I actually trained many years ago, as discussed earlier. John remembers how through trance mediumship sometimes I would speak with the voice of people such as Gandhi, Billy Fury (the British sixties pop star) and Elvis Presley. John didn't know at that time that I was a singer in my own right. Generally I sing a couple of Billy Fury and Elvis songs at my shows, songs that I am sure the reader will know well, such as 'Halfway to Paradise', Billy's big hit record, and usually at the end of the evening 'American Trilogy', which of course was a Presley classic.

John has always stated emphatically that when I am on stage singing it is not me but Billy Fury or Elvis coming through. I always smile and say it is just my voice, but the unusual thing is that, wherever I travel to demonstrate my gift as a medium and do sing, so many people in the audience come up and say the same thing as John, that it is Billy or Elvis and not me! Some people say that they have seen these stars standing behind me or next to me; others that it is almost like a strange mystical experience at those times. Certainly members of both stars' families who have listened to my voice have commented on certain similarities. I don't know really for myself, but if I am overshadowed or inspired by either of these wonderful men, Elvis Presley or Billy Fury, who were both very interested in psychic matters, the paranormal and the afterlife, I feel incredibly honoured.

I have also been very lucky to work with lots of other famous psychics, mediums and mystics in recent years, including my good friend Derek Acorah. We did quite a few shows together for Granada Breeze some years ago. Much of Derek's work for programmes such as *Most Haunted* was sometimes seen as a little theatrical, but that's what I feel the programme needed at that time and I can assure all concerned first and foremost that Derek Acorah is a fine and genuine Spiritualist medium. I shall never forget late in 2006 taking a bit of a busman's holiday and going to see Derek demonstrate mediumship at my local theatre, Wolverhampton's Grand Theatre. Every seat was sold out that evening and I sat with my wife in the middle of the stalls. Derek spotted me from the stage and insisted that I stood up. He then proceeded to introduce me to everyone, spoke of our friendship, and told the audience that I was the finest medium he had ever worked with. I feel that Derek is like me, a genuine medium, who is never afraid to praise others and tries to help people progress spiritually too.

I must also admit that it can be difficult at times when so many members of the public want to meet you, especially when you have just been on the radio or television, or have had a major feature written about you in one of the newspapers. And then, of course, there is my work as a feature writer for *Psychic News* and a psychic agony uncle for the *Wolverhampton Express & Star*. So many people now write in to ask if I can help them. Sometimes I get literally hundreds of letters, often without return postage, some asking for advice, some for private readings and others for healing. Unfortunately I never have the time to see all of them, but I always write back and offer to send distant healing for them, which works just as well as physical contact. I also suggest to these people that they should say a prayer to whatever or whomever they believe God to be. If they are an atheist, then they should pray to something, anything they like, that they think of as being good in the world, and I tell them that at the same time I will send my thoughts of distant healing towards them.

As you can imagine, sometimes I can feel totally overwhelmed by the sheer volume of letters with enquiries about Spiritualism, my work as a medium and the psychic world in general, and there are times when I post the last batch of replies and say, "Guided by the Light and natural-born medium? Forget it! That's it - no more!" Hmm - famous last words, I think, and tomorrow is always another day! Born mediums never retire; Spirit doesn't let us until our work in this world, proving to others that there is no such thing as death, comes to its physical conclusion and it is time for us to join our loved ones on the other side.